SEVEN CHURCHES

LETTER TO THE BODY OF CHRIST

Apostle Stephanie Parker

DEDICATION

I would like to dedicate this book to my mother and friend the late Janie Purcell~Shivers, to my great grandparents the late Bishop H.L. & Evangelist Lucille Clayton (founders of Clayton Temple holiness church, Macon, GA) for planting the foundational seeds of holiness and birthing the understanding of God's revelation in my life.

TABLE OF CONTENTS

INTRODUCTION

I n this modern day society, it seems as though the majority of professing Christians are readily embracing a more practical philosophy of ministry, while searching for worldwide unity. This approach has left most feeling ineffective in both their application and understanding of sound doctrine.

Titus 2:1-9 (KJV) But speak thou the things which become sound doctrine: ² That the aged men be sober, grave, temperate, sound in faith, in charity, in patience. ³ The aged women likewise, that they be in behaviour as becometh holiness, not false accusers, not given to much wine, teachers of good things; ⁴ That they may teach the young women to be sober, to love their husbands, to love their children, ⁵ To be discreet, chaste, keepers at home, good, obedient to their own husbands, that the word of God be not blasphemed. ⁶ Young men likewise exhort to be sober minded. ⁷ In all things shewing thyself a pattern of good works: in doctrine shewing uncorruptness, gravity, sincerity, ⁸ Sound speech, that cannot be condemned; that he that is of the contrary part may be ashamed, having no evil thing to say of you. ⁹ Exhort servants to be obedient unto their own masters, and to please them well in all things; not answering again;…

It is extremely necessary that we not only study the Word of God in order to understand sound doctrine; we must also look deeply into the examples of Christ's words to the seven churches in Asia Minor. The contents in these minor epistles should not just be viewed or read as Bible stories. They are just as applicable to the churches of today as they were to the early churches.

Christ's letters to the seven churches in Asia Minor offers the churches of today a vivid portrait of God's expectations, criticism and promises. These letters also allow the people of God to examine their current spiritual state and constantly evaluate their beliefs and activities. This ensures that each individual practices what Christ expects of His church.

The one ongoing application of these letters that yet holds just as firm today is the phrase that appears in each letter: *"he that has an ear let him hear what the Spirit says unto the Church". Revelation 2:29 (KJV)* This particular statement occurs seven times in other books in the Bible. It alerts the Body of Christ to wake up and pay attention. At this beckoning, Christ is about to make a very important and profound statement to the church.

Christ is walking in the midst of the churches today, acting as both Inspector and Judge. He's observing the outward actions and attitudes, as well as the hearts and motives of those within the Church. His findings may be summarized best in *Ephesians 4:18-19 (KJV)*. *[18] Having the understanding darkened, being alienated from the life of God through the ignorance that is in them, because of the blindness of their heart: [19] Who being past feeling have given themselves over unto lasciviousness, to work all uncleanness with greediness.*

The solution or Christ's recommendation to the Church of today is found in *Ephesians 4:20-32 (KJV) [20] But ye have not so learned Christ; [21] If so be that ye have heard him, and have been taught by him, as the truth is in Jesus: [22] That ye put off concerning the former conversation the old man, which is corrupt according to the deceitful lusts; [23] And be renewed in the spirit of your mind; [24] And that ye put on the new man, which after God is created in righteousness and true holiness. [25] Wherefore putting away lying, speak every man truth with his neighbour: for we are members one of another. [26] Be ye angry, and sin not: let not the sun go down upon your wrath: [27] Neither give place to the devil. [28] Let him that stole steal no more: but rather let him labour, working with his hands the thing which is good, that he may have to give to him that needeth. [29] Let no corrupt communication proceed out of your mouth, but that which is good to the use of edifying, that it may minister grace unto the hearers. [30] And grieve not the holy Spirit of God, whereby ye are sealed unto the day of redemption. [31]*

Let all bitterness, and wrath, and anger, and clamour, and evil speaking, be put away from you, with all malice: ³² *And be ye kind one to another, tenderhearted, forgiving one another, even as God for Christ's sake hath forgiven you.*

The letters that John wrote to each of the seven churches in Asia Minor revealed the strengths and weaknesses of each church. We can, from their introspection, measure ourselves against the positive and negative aspects of our local body of believers. John's writing also reveals the mind of Christ concerning sufferings, false doctrine, love, lethargy and many other characteristics.

John declares that blessed is he that reads and hears the words of this prophecy and keeps the things which are written therein. *Revelation 1:3 (KJV) ³ Blessed is he that readeth, and they that hear the words of this prophecy, and keep those things which are written therein: for the time is at hand.* This should serve as a true blessing and encouragement to know that Christ himself is walking in the midst of the believers and is intimately acquainted with our every thought, word, motive and deed.

John's writing to the churches of Asia opens with salutations of grace and peace from God, the seven Spirits which are before His throne and from Jesus Christ, who is the faithful witness. These salutations soon turn our attention to the part of God's character, many believers seldom experience and many preachers seldom expound upon. God calls the churches Asia into question in a very judgmental way, portraying every failure of each church.

God never gives a problem without first supplying a solution. After John exposes the problems facing each of the seven churches, he then gives the call to repentance and zealousness. Regardless of where we are individually in our spiritual walk, whether we be well intentioned but still falling short; blind and compromising or even busy and loveless the message of Christ is one of hope, restoration and possibilities.

Did John only write to these seven churches? Hundreds of churches existed all over the world (approximately sixty-three years after the day of Pentecost). Why were these seven churches selected and recorded in history. John, the Prophet, clearly states his position as he pens these letters to the seven churches. *Revelation 1:9-11 (KJV)* *⁹ I John, who also am your brother, and companion in tribulation, and in the kingdom and patience of Jesus Christ, was in the isle that is called Patmos, for the word of God, and for the testimony of Jesus Christ. ¹⁰ I was in the Spirit on the Lord's day, and heard behind me a great voice, as of a trumpet, ¹¹ Saying, I am Alpha and Omega, the first and the last: and, What thou seest, write in a book, and send it unto the seven churches which are in Asia; unto Ephesus, and unto Smyrna, and unto Pergamos, and unto Thyatira, and unto Sardis, and unto Philadelphia, and unto Laodicea.*

The seven churches of Asia Minor are as follows:

Ephesus – the church that had forsaken its first love;

Smyrna – the church that would suffer persecution;

Pergamos – the church that needed to repent;

Thyatira – the church that had a false prophetess;

Sardis – the church that had fallen asleep;

Philadelphia – the church that endured patiently; and

Laodicea – the church with lukewarm faith.

The seven churches God selected represented the seven basic methods of Satan's attacks, dividing the Church or causing divisions among the individuals within the Church. The Spirit of division has a strong hold on the church because many believers are promoting carnality within denominational structures and have become narrow in their beliefs. Clergy have resisted the voice of the true prophets and have taken on a more patriotic approach to the gospel, depending solely upon the voice of the compromising prophets. Churches have lost their focus and have become more self-centered than Christ centered; more religious than righteous; more legalistic than loving; more elitist than encouraging; and certainly more traditional than truthful.

The Apostle Paul wrote very specifically warning the Body of Christ, at Corinth, against the divisions occurring among the saints. *1 Corinthians 1:10-13 (KJV) 10 Now I beseech you, brethren, by the name of our Lord Jesus Christ, that ye all speak the same thing, and that there be no divisions among you; but that ye be perfectly joined together in the same mind and in the same judgment. 11 For it hath been declared unto me of you, my brethren, by them which are of the house of Chloe, that there are contentions among you. 12 Now this I say, that every one of you saith, I am of Paul; and I of Apollos; and I of Cephas; and I of Christ. 13 Is Christ divided? was Paul crucified for you? or were ye baptized in the name of Paul?*

The greater message to the churches at Corinth, the seven churches of Asia Minor and the Churches of today is that the Word of God encourages Christian unity. Such divisions and schisms should not occur within the Christian community as it only serves to weaken the Church influence and her ability to draw those who are without Christ.

Paul's letter to the Church of God at Corinth, opens much like John's letter to the seven Churches in Asia Minor. The similarities prove that God's message is not only to the Church at Corinth or the seven churches of Asia Minor, but also to the universal church. When determining these prophetic sayings, one should note that the one church of Christ is made up of many local churches worldwide.

John's counsel to the seven churches of Asia Minor and to the Body of Christ today as well is for the Church to return back to her first love. He further encourages the church not fear in the face of persecution, to return to God's word, to stop compromising, to wake up, to be strong, to be rich in Christ, to be clothed in His righteousness, to be zealous, and to open the door anytime Christ knocks. *Luke 21:36 (KJV) [36] Watch ye therefore, and pray always, that ye may be accounted worthy to escape all these things that shall come to pass, and to stand before the Son of man.*

The Body of Christ has become the most underestimated people on earth. Non-Christians and even new Christians should not be expected to understand all spiritual things that pertain to Christianity. *1 Corinthians 3:1 (KJV) And I, brethren, could not speak unto you as unto spiritual, but as unto carnal, even as unto babes in Christ.*

Unfortunately, the judgment of the world against the church has also become the indictment of Christians against one another. We do in some instances take our liberty for granted. We have criticized our wrong, misused our power, neglected our goodness and forgotten about our significance to the Body of Christ. Thank God that Jesus thinks more of us then we think of ourselves. Jesus cares for us so that He is always giving us warnings and opportunities to get it right before destructions hits.

Proverbs 16:14-18 (KJV) ¹⁴ *The wrath of a king is as messengers of death: but a wise man will pacify it.* ¹⁵ *In the light of the king's countenance is life; and his favour is as a cloud of the latter rain.* ¹⁶ *How much better is it to get wisdom than gold! and to get understanding rather to be chosen than silver!* ¹⁷ *The highway of the upright is to depart from evil: he that keepeth his way preserveth his soul.* ¹⁸ *Pride goeth before destruction, and an haughty spirit before a fall.*

Isaiah 58:1 (KJV) Cry aloud, spare not, lift up thy voice like a trumpet, and shew my people their transgression, and the house of Jacob their sins.

Hebrews 7:25 (KJV) Wherefore he is able also to save them to the uttermost that come unto God by him, seeing he ever liveth to make intercession for them.

The purpose of this book is to expose the work of Satan against the church and to alert every reader to recognize the potential dangers of not heeding the warnings of God. *Isaiah 58:1 (RSV) "Cry aloud, spare not, lift up your voice like a trumpet; declare to my people their transgression, to the house of Jacob their sins..* John's epistles to the churches of Asia Minor served much of the same purpose. Merely doing church work and keeping religious traditions are not enough to please God. The seven churches were praised, criticized, and corrected at the same time. Ephesus forsook her first love; Smyrna suffered persecution; Pergamus needed to repent; Thyatira had a false prophetess; Sardis had fallen asleep; Philadelphia endured patiently and Laodicea became lukewarm in her faith.

As we prepare to embark upon our journey through those seven churches my question to my readers is "what church do you attend?" My question does not pertain to you physical place of worship, but rather how you worship. *John 4:24 (KJV)* *24 God is a Spirit: and they that worship him must worship him in spirit and in truth.*

ACKNOWLEGEMENTS

First giving honor to the glory of God the Father, God the Son and God the Holy Spirit, without whom this book would not be possible.

My husband, my boyfriend, my lover and Pastor James Parker, I love you for your love, prayers, patience and support during this time of preparation.

My children, Yualunda (Shawn) Gormley, La'kilah (Vernon), Sh~yvonne, Ja~ymez, Angel, my three grandsons Alan, Syrr and Izaac, and my god-daughters Organdy and Lashonna for believing and encouraging me to persevere.

To my dearest friends and mentors Bishop David and Evangelist Barnela Tabb, Pastors of House of Prayer church, Centerville, Ill. You spoke life in the most desolate times of my life. I'm very much grateful in your obedience to God.

Finally, to my Pastor, Chief Apostle Vertise and his lovely companion Pastor elect-lady Linda Rozier, (Cathedral of Faith) whom I love very much. Thank you for everything.

CHAPTER ONE
History on the Church of Ephesus, The Loveless Church (Revelations 2:1-7 KJV)

Ephesus means "my darling, my desired one" was the great metropolis of Asia Minor. The church at Ephesus was surrounded by materialism, paganism, heathenism and immorality. Perhaps the most significant reason for the prominence of Ephesus was religion. The Ephesians promoted the worship of Artemis during the Roman period, by minting coins with the inscription, "Diana of Ephesus." The Temple of Diana also contained a banking center in its great vault, which was considered the safest place in Asia Minor. The goddess Diana was the key for religious worship, "Great is Diana of the Ephesians (Acts 19:34b KJV)" She was the patron of all prostitutes and represented fertility and sexuality. The temple of Artemis, Diana's, Roman name, at Ephesus ranked as one of the Seven Wonders of the Ancient World. This temple at Ephesus housed the multi-breasted image of Artemis which was reputed to have come directly from Zeus (Acts 19:35 KJV).

Accompanied by Priscilla and Aquila, the Apostle Paul founded the church at Ephesus (Acts 18:18-22 KJV). During Paul's stay in Ephesus he encountered both great opportunities and great dangers. Shortly after the establishment of this church, wicked men attempted to imitate the Apostle Paul's special gifts. But such signs were soon proven to be counterfeit, and the Word of God grew and prevailed in the city (Acts 19:8-20 KJV). Paul baptized believers who accepted the gospel through the disciples of John the Baptist (19:1-5 KJV), and he encountered strong influences of magic (Act19:11-20 KJV). One of the things that characterized the early church, but not some of the other churches, was the refusal to fraternize with loose Christians. Yet Paul knew false teachers, wolves in sheep clothing's, would linger, ready to destroy the work of God. So Paul sounded an alarm warning the Church of Ephesus that grievous wolves will enter, not sparing the flock. Therefore watch, and remember (Acts 20:29-31 KJV). Matthew wrote; "Beware of false prophets, who come to you in sheep's clothing, but inwardly they are ravenous wolves" (Matthew 7:15 KJV).

Since this Christian assembly was taught by Paul, Apollo, Timothy, and John, it had been extremely well taught. This church ended the New Testament era considered one of the largest and greatest churches of the era, because of their fervent evangelism which helped convert many Jews. Even with the modern means of communication and travel today, we are unable to equal their evangelical success.

Ephesus Admirations

Christ praises those in the church at Ephesus for several qualities. In spite of their surroundings, they were active, energetic, patient, enduring, steadfast, and sensitive to the presence of evil, evildoers and impostors. Doctrinally, they were competent and militant in their stand against false teaching. The operation of spiritual discernment kept them pure, without compromising or theological error. They heeded the injunctions of the Holy Spirit to "watch out for those who may cause division and place obstacles in the way that was contrary to the teachings they had learned. "Now I urge you, brethren, note those who cause divisions and offenses, contrary to the doctrine that had been learned, and avoid them" (Roman 16:17 KJV). Church discipline is almost unheard of today. These believers were neither lazy nor idle but zealous of good works and service for the Lord. They spent their time working diligently and therefore growing weary as a result of their labors. Despite the fatigue from their labors, they were persistent in doing that which they knew needed to be accomplished. They condemned that which was morally wrong and kept them pure from immorality despite the fact that licentious behavior surrounded them.

The church of Ephesus was an assembly that withheld such a positive reputation that Christ saluted the Church of Ephesus with grace and peace. He was intimately aware of their thoughts and attitudes. These saints exemplified the word trust; they trusted God, consistently under trial. No matter how the Ephesian Christians were beaten down, discouraged, or persecuted, they did not quit. The intimate fellowship and love for the Lord Jesus Christ was essential in experiencing the abundance in their Christian life.

Christ's Complaints about Ephesus

Nevertheless, a shifting from praise to complaints against the church began to take place. Mohammedanism began to sweep through the land, destroying the once mighty church that Paul created. Also, the Ephesians' church was a prophetic picture of the apostolic church that eventually opened the door for legalism. Jesus walked among this church with eyes as a flame of fire esteeming Ephesus with praises; he finds a fatal fault. Despite such admirable works, all excellent programs, efforts and the church appearing to be perfect from the outside, Christ knew their hearts, and something was missing. Nevertheless, I have somewhat against thee; they had departed from their earlier heartfelt affection for the Lord! They no longer had that deep devotion and commitment in their hearts for Him as well as the love that fueled their motivation for service. The old abounding joy, gladness and enthusiasm began to wane. The services of the Church of Ephesus became mechanical and routine. The old flame and fire had diminished; they became cold and regular. The Ephesians' Believers begin to consist of callous Christians. They worked hard for the cause of Christ as contended for the faith and fought for doctrinal purity, but they lacked yieldedness to him due to their waning love for Christ.

The church of Ephesus could not realize its need to possess a love for Christ again unless it first acknowledged their love or passion was missing. The Lord commanded them to "remember" (vs.5)-"Remember therefore from whence thou art fallen; repent and do the first works, or else." Jesus clearly pointed out the most severe consequence of disobedience. Formalism had crept into Ephesus. This was the time they needed to recall the joy of their salvation, the psalmist David prayed: "Restore to me the joy of my salvation, and uphold me by your generous Spirit. Then I will teach transgressors your ways and sinners shall convert to you." (Psalm 51:12, 13 KJV). Also, they needed to accept they were too busy serving and not taking time for sweet fellowship at the feet of Jesus. Luke 10 tells the story of Mary and her sister, Martha. Jesus said to Martha, You are worried and troubled about many things. But one thing is needed, and Mary has chosen that good part (vs.41, 42 KJV). When one is so active with missionary endeavors and good works there is no time for a personal relationship with Christ, this is considered too busy and is heading toward a great fall. Before realizing, service organizations, committees and programs has become first in many lives. Multitudes have fallen to this indictment. When first saved the people of God loved Jesus, loved to pray, loved to read the Word, loved to attend the services at God's house and loved to witness. What has happen to the zeal? They have lost their first love; they not only have become spiritually weak, but they cease winning souls.

If the love for Christ Jesus was what it should be, no act of service is too small, no task is too great, no sacrifice too much for Him. Dr. M.R. DeHaan, the great prophetic Bible teacher, once stated,

"To come to Christ costs nothing, to follow Christ costs something, but to serve Christ cost everything."

Jesus said,
"Whoever finds his life will lose it, and whoever loses his life for my sake will find it" (Matthew 10:39 KJV).

Religion has taken preeminence over relationship. The church of today needs to do what David did, and do it quickly! We should have a fear of losing God's spirit and being rejected by God.

The Judge then commanded the Church of Ephesus to "repent" or else, an act of the mind will determine a change in behavior and attitude. Repent is not something you do at conversion and then quit. Repent is something you do to perpetually clean your life to stay in a relationship with Christ. Repent, to the highest level, return to the highest level, where God is the primary and not secondary in the Believers lives. God wants a church that loves him passionately. They needed to know if they desired to have that same love once again. Take action to change those negative behaviors and return to God. "Do the first works" the simple faith in Jesus Christ and a genuine love for Him or what He had done. Paul writes; "wherefore, my beloved, as ye have always obeyed, not as in my presence only, but now much more in my absence, work out your own salvation with fear and trembling"(Philippians 2:12 KJV).

The leaders of the church of Ephesus judged false prophets in the earlier days but became lax as they lost their first love. Today many think it's wrong to judge heresy or wickedness. NOT SO! The same God who said, "Judge not, that ye be judged" (Matthew 7:1 KJV) also declared, "Judge righteous judgment" (John 7:24 KJV). A believer is never to judge based on characters or motives. However, he should definitely judge when an individual's doctrine is heretical or his life is filled with wickedness. The Apostle Paul taught, "He who is spiritual judges all things" (1Corinthians 2:15 KJV). Those who are truly spiritual will not accept something at face value. They will judge it according to Scripture to determine whether it is the Holy Spirit's work, before accepting it or becoming involved. We can judge a teaching, prophetic utterance or any other supposedly spiritual act by the anointing of God.

Satan has kept many of the Body of Christ from obeying God. Because the people say you are judging them. 1st Corinthians 2:15 1a states, "But he that is spiritual judgeth all things."

The Believers must try (proving and examining) every spirit as the scriptures teach (1John 4:1KJV).

They must also as Christians examine and determine its soundness. By not accepting anything without judging it, this will assist Christians from the possibility of deception or any erroneous spirits at work against the church. A True church is a church in the world, but not of the world.

Many Fundamentalists today are valiantly contending for the faith and fighting one battle after another; but for some, their motivation for service falls short; Love for their Savior is no longer behind their preaching, teaching and contending for the Faith. The service of God has become a game for many believers, it's all about a personal gain, and anything goes. People of God once had Morals that were upheld. Now Godly principles and talk about living Godly, is no longer a required standard according to many churches today, but acting as if they are religious, yet rejecting the power that could make them Godly is (2Timothy 3:5 NLT). "Everyone should have a standard, but most of these standards do not incorporate the fundamentals of God. Many are forever learning, but are never able to come to the knowledge of the truth." (2Timothy3:7 KJV). Seeking after the kingdom of God is not first, but materialistic, fame and fortune is. As Matthew 6:33 KJV clearly states; "But seek ye first the kingdom of God, and his righteousness; and all these things shall be added unto you. When our priority is spiritual, God will take care of the material, for where God guides, He provides."

It is certainly easy to become so caught up in the battle, that a proper perspective and motivation for service is lost, but Godly, Bible-believing Fundamentalist churches today need to especially take heed to Christ's message to the church of Ephesus; Outward "good works" means little to Christ if one is serving Him for the wrong reason.

If the body of believers have lost their first love, have wrong confession, false doctrines, false teachers, spiritual death, fear and loss of spiritual power they are displeasing to God.

Consequences/Promises

The consequences of failing to heed Christ's counsel were serious. Christ said the Church of Ephesus would lose its influence to the point it would become nonexistent as a light in the midst of darkness (v.5). Don't let this happen to you. Even today, any work not motivated by love for the Savior is empty and futile. First Corinthians 13:1-3 KJV further reveals the importance of love as the impetus for service. Fundamentalist ministries today who seek to preach or teach and contend for the faith should carefully consider and evaluate their own reasons for service to Christ. Is it for worldly gain or heavenly fame?

Christ promises an eternal reward for those who overcome, to eat of the tree of life in the midst of the Paradise of God, "Tree of Life". The Love for Christ is the proper motivation for Christian service. Stand the test of your love. The Lord Jesus said, "By their fruit you will know them" (Matthew 7:16 KJV).

The question was asked; who is an overcomer? When one accepts Jesus, he overcomes Satan; by the power of the Holy Spirit, God's Word and the blood of the Lamb, the overcomer always succeeds! Jesus said, "I have overcome the world (John16:33 KJV). Who is it that overcomes the world? He who believes Jesus is the Son of God. Overcoming the world is the experience that takes place in the life of the individual who puts his or her faith in Jesus Christ. For Paul said, "No, despite all these things, overwhelming victory is ours through Christ, who loved us" (Romans 8:37 NLT).

It's noted the Believers need to take heed to this message, for there are many false Prophets going about disguised as servants of Jesus Christ but who are really enemies of the cross, seeking their own personal gain. The ecclesiastical sickness of "ecumania" (a one-world church regardless of one's faith), has caught the attention of many church leaders. "If you love me, you will obey what I command" (John 14:15 KJV).

The Body of Believers should choose to believe what God's Word says and accept the truth. Today's Christians have no excuse. Let the words of Christ, in all their richness, live in your hearts and make you wise (Colossians 3:16 NLT).

"He that hath an ear let him hear what the Spirit says unto the churches."

CHAPTER TWO
Smyrna, The Persecuted Church
(Revelations 2:12-13 KJV)

The city of Smyrna was often called the "glory of Asia" because of its idyllic harbor and exceptional temples and architecture. It was also known to be the wealthy and commercial center of Asia Minor. Its name was received from the trading of Smyrna. Smyrna in Greek means (myrrh). Myrrh was one-half of the anointing oil and its total purpose was to take pain away.

Myrrh was the principal ingredient in the anointing oil (Exodus 30:23a KJV), when the church was crushed with trials; the fragrance of her faith was released. Myrrh was also used as a painkiller as well as a spicy fragrance for the anointing of dead bodies. Jesus was offered Myrrh on the cross at Calvary, but refused because he knew it would take the pain away and extend his time of suffering. It exhibits the suffering of our Lord for our sins.

The Jewish segment of the population seemed to have been most irreligious and neglectful of spiritual things. They worshipped Caesar and were home to large Jewish communities who were Jews by nationality only. Smyrna was a city full of hatred against Christians. The church at Smyrna was plagued by severe physical persecution at the hands of evil men and false teachers within the city who were fueled by the Jewish community, who hated the followers of Christ. This community not only persecuted Christians physically, but also boycotted their businesses, leaving them financially destitute. Scribes and Pharisees considered them to be unlearned, untaught, and unschooled men of poor and deprived lives. Also the Jews incited the Pagans in the city to unlawfully loot the possessions of the Christians and drive them into hiding. "Those things gain to me; those are counted loss for Christ" (Philippians 3:7 KJV). Paul willingly renounced all his earthly advantages and Jewish privileges as a means of attaining salvation. The church of Smyrna was the most faithful church in the face of persecution. Their true faith could not be destroyed, but the process of refining faith through their trials was through God.

Polycarp, the pastor of the church of Smyrna was taken by Roman Soldiers at the age of 86 and was told to say "Lord Caesar" his refusal to say "Lord Caesar" caused him to be burned alive in the Public Square. The Smyrna Christians were also fed to the lions at Rome while multitudes cheered. Satan unleashed a violent attack on the church in an effort to obliterate it, for it became evident to him the apostolic church, because of its faithful preaching of the gospel, had become a serious threat to his worldwide godless empire.

History informs us that approximately tens of millions may have been martyred during this era. Their faithful works performed in the name of Jesus, brought great tribulation and accompanying poverty. The Church of Smyrna probably suffered the greatest persecution in all Christianity. Their earthly trials constituted a problem of their salvation, but their suffering was only for a season, or temporary.

Smyrna was the proudest of all the cities of Asia Minor. God was not supreme. To Smyrna, the glories of Greek culture and worldly things were supreme. Diocletian was considered the worst emperor in Rome's history and the greatest antagonist of the Christian Faith. He also led a violent attempt to destroy the Bible from the face of the earth. The spirit within Diocletian is still roaming in the world today, when a woman by the name of Madeline Murray was successful in her fight to have prayer removed from the schools. Where were the Christians?

Christ's Consolation

Christ introduced Himself as "the first and the last, or Alpha and Omega, who was dead, and is alive" (Revelation 2:8 KJV). "I know thy works, and tribulation, and poverty, but thou art rich. I know the blasphemy of them who say they are Jews, and are not, but are the synagogue of Satan" (Revelation 2:9 KJV). God knew the heart of every one who were afflicting the Children of God and knew they were persecuted falsely in the name of religion. For the word of God states; "but even if you suffer for doing what is right, God will reward you for it. "So don't be afraid and don't worry" (1Peter 3:15 NLT). The unique characteristic of Christians is that they do not worship as dead man, as do the Muslims, the Buddhists, or Daddy Grace, but a Christ who is alive.

The church of Smyrna's persecution came through false professors of religion, those who said they were Jews, ones whose heart was right with God. And true circumcision was not a cutting of the body but a change of heart produced by God's Spirit. "Who seeks praises from God, not from people" (Romans 2:29 NLT) but in reality, they were not! They were actually members of the synagogue of Satan because they denied the deity of Christ.

"Every spirit that confessed not that Jesus Christ is come in the flesh is not of God (1John 4:3 KJV), as well as, those who mix law and grace. Paul says, "I marvel that ye are so soon removed from him that called you into the grace of Christ unto another gospel. Which is not another, but there be some that trouble you, and would pervert the gospel of Christ. But though we, or an angel from heaven, preach unto you, let him be accursed. As we said before, so say I now again, If any man preach any other gospel unto you than that ye have received, let him be accursed" (Galatians1:6-9 KJV).

Christ, who himself had conquered death, promises Smyrna Christian's that if they should stay faithful to Him even unto death, they will receive the crown of life (Revelation 2:10 KJV). Look at those in the scripture who were in the perfect Will of God that suffered. Daniel a prisoner of war for 70 years, was sent to the lion's den because of his prayer life, Paul was beheaded by the command of Nero, who also ordered Peter to be crucified upside down, Domitian, who ordered John exiled, Trajan, who had Ignatius the second pastor of Antioch fed alive to the lions in the coliseum.

God promises the overcomer, even if they suffered a physical death, will not suffer the "second death," another phrase for eternal death, or spending eternity in the lake of fire and separated from God. Paul states, "For I reckon that the sufferings of this present time are not worthy to be compared with the glory which shall be revealed in us" (Roman8:18 KJV).

"Temptation is one of the enemy's most powerful "schemes" for misleading God's people" (Ephesians 6:11,16 KJV). In the face of such satanic opposition, Christ's message was …. "Fear none of those things which thou shall suffer" and "be thou faithful unto death (v10)." "Keep your eyes on the eternal reward", according to James 1:12 KJV: "Blessed is the man that endures temptation for when he is tried, he shall receive the crown of life, which the Lord hath promised to them that love him." G. Campbell Morgan noted that in this instance:

"Silence is more eloquent than all language."

The conduct and the character of this church of Smyrna perfectly satisfied the Savior. That he had not one complaint about this church.

Could this be said about the church of today? It is strongly believed the church of today would not be able to endure persecution as the church of Smyrna endured. The church of today hasn't conquered the tests of someone not speaking to them; the funny looks/rolling of the eyes, the lies that are told, scandalizing or just the negative things said about them from those they have sweet counsel with. My former Apostle Dr. Teresa Martin would frequently say,

> *"If you can't endure the tests of this life, don't expect the trials and you can forget the tribulations."*

To simplify this, if you can't take the heat then you should get out of the kitchen, or in better terms; no endurance no blessings. Spiritual maturity is in such great demand today, but this will only come from applying God's word to our daily lives.

This question is often asked, "If God is so good, then why does he allow such things as temptations and suffering to happen in the first place?" John Hagee states in his Book of The Apocalypse:

> *"It's the sovereign plan and purposes of God. God's long-range plan you do not have the mental ability to see or comprehend."*

But scripture clearly reveals to us that temptation can be overcome. "Remember that the temptations that come into your life are no different from what others experience. And God is faithful. He will keep temptation from becoming so strong you can't stand up against it. When you are tempted, he will show you a way out so that you will not give in to it" (1Corinthians 10:13 NLT). (1Peter 4:13 KJV) states, "Beloved, think it not strange concerning the fiery trial which is to try you, as though some strange thing happened unto you, But rejoice, inasmuch as ye are partakers of Christ's sufferings; that, when his glory shall be revealed, ye may be glad also with exceeding joy."

Christ's Counsel

Faithful believers today have no need to fear, for they will receive the approval of our Savior and assurance of escaping the lake of fire (Revelation 20:11-15 KJV).

Christ likewise exhorts his children today to diligently honor and serve Him at all costs. "Store up for yourself treasures in heaven" (Matthew 6:20 KJV). Believers must know why they believe what they believe and remain rooted and grounded in faith (1 Peter 3:14 KJV). They must also realize that God often allows suffering in order to make the believer more suitable for the Master's use. As (Philippians1:29 KJV) states: "For unto you it is given in the behalf of Christ, not only to believe on him, but also to suffer for his sake."

"Forasmuch then as Christ hath suffered for us in the flesh, arm yourselves likewise with the same mind: for he that hath suffered in the flesh hath ceased from sin; that he no longer should live the rest of his time in the flesh to the lusts of men, but to the will of God" (1Peter 4:1-2 KJV). Paul writes, "in order for him to know Christ: that he might both experience His resurrection power and share in His sufferings, and thus he would be more and more conformed to His death" (Philippians 3:10 KJV).

We as the church of today, should all want to know the righteousness of God so that we can obtain a personal relationship with God, because companionship in sorrow establishes the most intimate and lasting ties, as afflicted hearts cling to each other.

The church of today must be aware that in the midst of trials and temptations, the manner in which you respond is vitally important. Also your confession is extremely important, because you confess who you are to be as calling those things, which are not as though they were (Roman 4:17 KJV). "Faith has to have a valid content. Confess what the word says in order to create an atmosphere in which God's works can lift you above your circumstances." Example, "I am an overcomer!" We as believers need to use such times of difficulty to honor and glorify Christ who suffered and died for all" (1Peter 4:12-16 KJV). Be persistent in your praise. Praises move God to a sense of urgency in your deliverance. "Faithful perseverance through trials will bring a crown of life" (James 1:12 KJV). Don't misunderstandably look on tragedies as a curse of God; for trials are however, the means through which God's blessings can come. Again notice the emphasis upon hearing the Spirit of God.

"He that hath an ear let him hear what the spirit says unto the churches" (Matthew 11:15).

CHAPTER THREE
The Worldly Church (Pergamos)
(Revelations 2:8-11 KJV)

Pergamos (or Pergamum) means "mixed marriage," a perverted marriage, or a commingling with the world. The name Pergamos has in it the root from which we got the English words _bigamy_ and _polygamy_. This was a crime and practice of having two or more wives/husbands at the same time.

Pergamos was the capital of Asia Minor; a pagan center of idolatry, demonic religions and home to the imperial cult which centered around the worship of Caesar, the Roman emperor. The church Pergamos became infested with self-indulgence, materialism, and worldliness. It also contained several notable temples to pagan gods and goddesses. It was the site of the altar to Zeus (Latin-Jupiter) the head of all the gods, Athena (the god of wisdom), and Dionysius (the god of wine and of drama). The most prominent religious systems of this city were the worship of Bacchus (the god of revelry) and the worship of Asclepius (the god of healing). Asclepius' emblem was a serpent. Snakes roamed freely around in the temple and wickedness spread through Pergamos like a brushfire.

Pergamos was the place where the nerves of the political, social, and state religion, branch out through all Asia Minor. "God said there is a very real Devil and his main purpose is to steal, kill and destroy you" (John 10:10 KJV). When Lucifer fell, and was kicked out of heaven, he kept his brilliance. He came down to this earth and he set up his throne. Although Satan fueled the persecution of the church at Smyrna, he chose Pergamos as his seat of Power, his throne, and the place where he would dwell.

Inspired by Satan through Nimrod and his mother, idolatry gained its start in Babylon, which was the capital of this kingdom. As long as Babylon was a dominant world power, it made an excellent headquarters for Satan's attack on the human race. That was the reason behind Satan's selection of Pergamos, because it was a strong idolatrous religion. Being in an area where Satan's manifestation was evident caused the Christians to be in a weakened position. From there Satan directed the affairs of his worldwide kingdom, perverting the souls of human beings.

In this Satan used "religion" and false teaching as his own individual work focus was to infiltrate such a world system into the church so it would lure unsuspecting individuals away from a relationship with God.

During this Pergamum age, many outstanding leaders were produced in the ceremonies of paganism which later were supported by artificial doctrines of an unscriptural nature who went on to pollute the true doctrine of the church.

It was during this time the Arian controversy was fought at the council of Nicea. Arius and his followers denied the personal deity of our Savior. Their concept of Christ was much like that of the modern-day Jehovah's Witness. Dr. H.A. Ironside, in his book "Lectures on the Book of Revelation", tells this story:

> "At the point, the brilliant Arius seemed almost to have stopped all opposition when a hermit from the deserts of Africa sprang to his feet, clad chiefly in the tiger's skin. This later he tore from his back, disclosing great scars (the result of having been thrown into the arena among the wild beasts). With his back dreadfully disfigured by animal claws exposed to their view, he dramatically cried, "These are the brand marks of the Lord Jesus Christ, and I cannot hear this Blasphemy." Then he proceeded to give so stirring an address, setting forth clearly the truth as to Christ's eternal deity, that the majority of the council realized in a moment that it was indeed the voice of the Holy Spirit."

2 Dr. Ironside continues,

Whether this story is actually true or not, I cannot say; but it sets forth the spirit pervading many who participated in the council, most of whom had passed through the terrible persecution of Diocletian. The final outcome of the Council of Nicea was that Jesus Christ was declared to be "very God of very God," "perfection of perfection," and God and man in one person.

The Doctrine Of Balaam

What was the doctrine of Balaam? Who was Balaam? Balaam was a magician or soothsayer who was summoned by the Moabite King Balak to curse the Israelites. After the Lord specifically instructed him to go to Balak, the exact meaning of the account of Balaam's "stubborn" donkey was not clear. The angel of the Lord blocked their way; the donkey balked three times and was beaten by Balaam, who had not seen the angel. Finally, after the third beating, the donkey spoke, reproving Balaam.

Balaam also taught Balak to entice the Israelites to sin by eating food sacrificed to idols and by committing sexual immorality (Numbers 25:1,2 KJV).

In the book of Numbers Balak (the king of Moab) feared the children of Israel hired Balaam a "corrupt prophet who many believed had the power to "bless and curse," To prophesy a curse against Israel. Balaam refused to curse instead persuaded Balak to influence the people of Israel to curse themselves by making them believe that God's promises were unconditional and that the promises hold good whether they obey God or not. In other words do whatever you want to; God will forgive you anyway, just because of his grace. This is taught throughout many Churches of today. Satan changed his approach during this Pergamum period to one of indulgence and elevation because he knew he would never conquer the Christians by attacking them. Only through entice and influence would he cause them to operate in disobedience that would eventually lead there destruction.

The Pergamos church began to embrace the pleasures of the world and became a worldly church. They also heeded to false doctrine of the theology of Balaam.

Not only were they worldly, sinful, and idolatrous, but they also shared in the wicked practice of Nicolaitans (ecclesiastical Hitlerism) which came from two Greek words Niko, to conquer, or "lord over," and laos, which meant the common people. These were Church leaders who believed they had authority to "lord over" their congregations. The members had no voice in the affairs of the church, but were required to blindly obey the decrees of the leader. This is referred to as the hierarchical system of Church government. In Revelation 2:6 KJV, God says, "but this thou hast, that thou hatest the deeds of the Nicolaitans, which I also hate". This teaching is in operation today and has ruined many non-denominational churches.

Christ's Message To Pergamos

Christ's complaint centered on its lack of separation from those who espoused false teaching. While the corporate church body did not hold to false doctrine, some in the assembly did, and the church did not separate from them. When Paul says; "ye cannot drink the cup of the Lord, and the cup of the devils; ye cannot be partakers of the Lord's Table and of the table of the devils" (1Corinthians10:21 KJV). This is saying you cannot serve God and mammon, for either you will hate the one, and love the other (Matthew 6:24 KJV).

The Body of Christ has professed Christianity as a system of doctrine, but not as a rule of life by adapting to the world format. You can do anything you want, live any kind of way and yet be considered a Christian. That word Christian has become loose in the mouth of people.

Webster defines Christian as a follower of Christ. Christians were loyal to Christ. This name represents a name of honor and not of shame. Then why are the representatives of Christians not exemplifying the life of Christ?

The fascinating appearance of the world and what it has to offer has lured many believers in many things not of God. Peer pressure typically has driven the train toward sin…Can the Body of Christ consistently set the pattern for righteousness, which will set the people of God and those who observe the people of God to success? Or are we bound to a life of dibbling and dabbling in and out of the truth. By participating in the very things that we are yet to be delivered from hinders from their growth process concerning the matter at hand. Reckless regard for other's spiritual advancement happened then and is happening now.

The lust of the flesh is still producing fruit even today. The struggle continues to bring the body under subjection (1Corinthians 9:27 KJV), many believers still buffet their bodies, but it is obvious that the battle is not yet over, and victory is not yet secured. Sexual impurity is on the rampage. Fornication and adultery has become a game that is played not only in the world but in the Body of Christ as well. Many believers might say they are not committing fornication or adultery. Maybe or maybe not physical or naturally so, but look at the possibility of spiritually. Fornication is defined as sexual relationships outside the bonds of marriage, adultery is the willful sexual intercourse with someone other than one's spouse, in the physical aspect.

Now on the spiritual aspect;

When the people of Israel and Judah refused to obey God, or when they practiced Idolatry, the prophets accused them of committing spiritual adultery (Jeremiah 3: 6-10 KJV).

In the Book of Revelation, fornication is symbolic of how idolatry and pagan religion defiles the true worship of God. The lust of many believers' heart has defiled their intimacies with God. Lust has signified many believers' evil desire and sins. John writes; "for all that is in the world, the lust of the flesh, and the lust of the eyes, and the pride of life, is not of the Father, but is of the world" (1John 2:16 KJV). "Your worldly lust has become those of materialism and not of God, "your homes, cars, money, spouses, children, and jobs." "For I the Lord thy God is a jealous God" (Deuteronomy 5:9 KJV)." Upon this statement; can it truthfully be said the act of fornication and adultery is still not in existence in the body of Christ physically and spiritually?

Paul states; "be not conformed to this world: but be ye transformed" (Roman 12:2a KJV). The church of today is looking for easier ways to justify their unrighteous ways of living, instead of maintaining a faithful relationship with God. For the Bible clearly states; "for the time will come when they will not endure sound doctrine; but after their own lusts shall they heap to themselves teachers, having itching ears" (2Timothy 4:3 KJV).

The temptation to compromise and to embrace worldly values and behaviors is as much a threat to believers today as ever. Faithfulness, loyalty and dedication are words that are hardly found and are not valued among the believers anymore. It's hard to find believers or people in general who will uphold faithfulness, loyalty or dedication especially when it pertains to the House of God. Those words of honor require the Body of Christ to endure things the flesh won't submit to, not taking into consideration, that if they are faithful over a few things God will make thee ruler over many (Matthew 25:23 KJV). Can God depend on you?

The lack of perseverance has diminished. And the world has made it possible for endurance be unacceptable. If there is something you don't like don't except it, just get rid of it. If you are unhappy with your marriage don't work things out, just divorce, and if the preacher is teaching what you don't want to hear don't pray for them just find another church. If you are not treated fairly on your job, then quit. Where is the endurance? When the word of God clearly states:

"Thou therefore endure hardness, as a good soldier of Jesus Christ" (2Timothy 2:3 KJV).

Many of the Body of Christ has conformed to compromising and the acceptance of the excuse system. Its all right God understands. Wrong! This action of compromising and tolerance for error is greatly displeasing to the Lord and the refusal to take heed to God's Word or God's warning concerning this matter is a dangerous mistake. No man is able to stand before God and say he turned away from God because God did not give any light. All men have had the revelation of God; therefore, all men are accountable to Him and are without excuses (Roman 1:20 KJV).

The sincere Body of Christ has to compare themselves as a soldier, an athlete, and a farmer, playing according to the rules, the rule of training and endurance, all of which has suffered privation in order to be rewarded at the end.

It was once noted unless you are willing to repent for your violations of sins and return in obedience to the Word, you will be judged by the Word (vs.16). The Church of Pergamos was in need of confession of their sins and forgiveness or face God in the judgment, as well as, many believers today. "Also submitting yourself in this life even to your lusts that war in your members" (James 4:1 KJV). God's Word states; "submit yourselves therefore to God. Resist the devil, and he will flee from you. Draw nigh to God, and he will draw nigh to you. Don't take on the attitude of the Church of Pergamos, but cleanse your hands, ye sinners; and purify your hearts, ye double minded" (James4: 7&8).

God wanted Pergamos and many believers today to return to him even now so that he could satisfy them! They were in need of repentance or be judged by the Word of God. God's Word, represents the double-edge sword of the mouth of God.

Many of the people of God need to change their mind concerning who they will allow to remain in their fellowship and separate from those who embrace false doctrine. "They must also choose this day whom they will serve" (Joshua 24:15). And demonstrate they are yet faithful to their divine call and charge.

This does not leave room for dialogue or compromise. The Word of God is the standard by which man will be judged, and those who reject or twist the scriptures will do so only to their own destruction.

Fundamentalist, Bible believing Christians today must make sure they are not only doctrinally sound but also doctrinally pure in their fellowships.

Preach the word; be instant in season, and out of season; reprove, rebuke, exhort with all long-suffering and doctrine.

"He that hath an ear let him hear what the Spirit says unto the churches" (Matthew 11:15).

CHAPTER FOUR
Thyatira, The Paganized Church
(Revelation 2:18-29 KJV)

Thyatira which means "continual sacrifice" or "last work" was known for its manufacturing and commercial center. It was a wealthy city in Macedonia, noted in the ancient days for its dying wool industry. There was a temple for powerful female oracle who presided over a lucrative fortune-telling business in Thyatira.

Archaeologists were able to uncover evidence of many trade guilds and unions for Membership. It's financial and social success, often involved pagan customs and practices such as superstitions worship, union feasts and loose sexual morality.

This church of Thyatira also was known in history as the Church of the Dark Age. This period was the merging of paganism with Christianity, which began under the church of Pergamum. In that Dark Age period, and also today, the Universal Catholic Church headquartered in Rome gradually became more Babylonian than Christian. Thyatira was an apostate church, who looks upon herself as the infallible oracle of the almighty. Prophetically,

Seven Churches

Thyatira fit the church era that spanned the Middle Ages also, that bound the people to image worship, superstition and priest-craft. The light that was once entrusted from God to His Church all but flickered out during those periods of the Dark and Middle Ages and was not rekindled until the days of the Reformation.

However, the message still reached far beyond the immediate circumstances in the church of Thyatira. It's been suggested that the Ephesian Church evangelized Thyatira or perhaps Paul's first convert in Philippi, Lydia, a seller of Purple, of the city of Thyrtira, which worshipped God, when she heard us whose heart the Lord opened, that she attended unto the things which were spoken of Paul (Acts 16:14 KJV).

Thyatira, however, was loaded with meritorious service and unusual deeds. She was known for: (1) "faith;" (2) "love"; and a love for humankind, for hospitals and sanitariums were almost exclusively the work of the church through its nuns and priests; (3) "deeds", through Roman history had been faithfully serving God as a result receiving Him;(4) "service" ministry; (5) "perseverance" endurance; and (6) "works" for the good works of the Church of Rome, except during the period of the Inquisition, when many were wantonly murdered. The main characteristic of this church seemed to be of its "works" toward people rather than doctrinal belief. Although Thyatira had many admirable qualities, she nevertheless had some deep-rooted problems which interfered with their relationship with God as well. Thyatira was guilty of terrible sin and God hates sin. "Sin expresses itself in either an act or attitude. Sin causes the people of God to fall short of God's glory" (Roman 3:23 KJV), "sin causes people to go astray like a wandering

47

sheep" (Isaiah 53:6 KJV), "sin transgresses or overstep the law" (Psalm 51:1 KJV), "sin trespass or exercise people's own will in the realm of divine authority" (Ephesians 2:1 KJV). "Sin affects Destiny. Sin causes people to be lost" (Matthew 18:11) "and if not forgiven sin causes people to perish" (John 3:16 KJV). Sin also brings people to judgment (Luke 12:20 KJV). Sin affects the Will. When He announced His mission in the synagogue in Nazareth, He indicated one thing He came to do was to free the captives (Luke 4:18 KJV). Sin affects the body. This was an indication of the man who was healed at the Pool of Bethesda (John 5:14 KJV). And Sin affects others. The sins of the scribes affected widows and others who followed their traditions (Luke 20:46-47 KJV). Rest assured, judgment will always come: "and surely the sins of the peoples will find them out" (Numbers 32:23 KJV).

God's Criticism In Thyatira

To the angel of the church in Thyatira; these things saith the Son of God, who hath his eyes like unto a flame of fire (fire speaks of burning indignation and purifying judgment), and his feet are like fine brass (brass symbols the wrath of the judgment of God); "Notwithstanding I have a few things against thee, because thou sufferest that woman Jezebel, which callest herself a prophetess, to teach and to seduce my servants to commit fornication, and to eat things sacrificed unto idols" (Revelation 2:18&20 KJV).

God delivers His criticism, charging the church of Thyatira with tolerating the teachings of the false prophetess Jezebel. Their diversion from true worship of Jesus Christ the Son of God was so serious that it called for a reiteration of His deity. Who was this Jezebel? And what did she teach that angered God so?

Her name immediately takes us back to Israel. Ahab, the king married a daughter of the king of Sidon, whose name was Jezebel. She introduced her heathen gods unto Israel in its worst days of apostasy. She was a brilliant and zealous woman, who slew the prophets of Jehovah, swept Israel off its religious feet, and subverted the doctrine of God. Jezebel even brought the mighty prophet, Elijah, down to his knees as he fled before her face for his life and prayed that he might die. But who is this Jezebel of Thyatira who claims to be an oracle of God, a prophetess, and to deliver the infallible words of heaven and who teaches and seduces God's servants?

God refers to her teaching as "the depths of Satan." This prophetess delivers not the true message of God, but her own evil, corrupt doctrine. The sin of this self-appointed prophetess was to bring Baalism into Israel as a new religion. Jezebel was perhaps the wickedest woman of her day. The scriptures clearly state; "for there shall arise false Christ and false prophets, and shall show great signs and wonders; insomuch that, if it were possible, they shall deceive the very elect" (Matthew 24:24 KJV).

The false teachings of Jezebel entered into the truth of God and pervade it. When the church married the world many churches begin to suffer false teaching and did not put forth an effort to stop it. Nor did preachers get up in the pulpit and rebuke false, devilish teachings that false prophets brought into the churches; they basically just ignored it. Pastor Paula White once said in her message a Face–to-face Encounter; you can allow false teachers to come to your church, but don't allow false teachers to contaminate your church. Because once that bacteria festers its spread through your system (the system representing the church) and then it becomes a hard task to get that bacteria under control or destroyed.

Many religious leaders have wandered from the truth of the word of God. But unless truth is not being perverted, there can never be error. And teachers like Jezebel appear spiritual and always claim great insight in the things of God. However they deceived themselves, they are able to deceive others because of their abilities as teachers.

They have taken the Word of God and turned it, misinterpreting the scriptures to fit their beliefs, justifying their traditions and even to hold on to their unrighteous behaviors. But the scripture reads, "rightly divide the word of truth" (2 Timothy 2:15 KJV). In other words (cut it straight) regularly and systematically interpreting God's Word according to its proper meaning and not your opinion if the desire of God's will is to be in your lives.

"The Body of Christ needs to be watchful of such false apostles, deceitful workers, transforming themselves into the apostles of Christ" (2Corinthians 11:13 KJV). "Because a false witness will utter lies" (Proverbs 14:5b KJV).

The long-suffering and loving God gave Thyatira ample time to do right and they resisted, like many of the Christians today are constantly rejecting the Wooing of the blessed Holy Spirit.

This woman also almost subverts all Christendom by seducing God's servants into committing sexual immoralities (fornicating with the devil). All kinds of ungodly sexual action were going on at that time. And those same actions are going on today. This has become a serious problem. What is the church, the Body of Believers, Christians, Saints or the Body of Christ doing about it?

The Apostle Paul gave us a glimpse of how a society would utterly slip into the degrading condition of sexual perversion. Paul writes in the book of Romans,

1. "For this reason God gave them over to degrading passion; for their women exchanged the natural function for that which is unnatural, and in the same way also the men abandoned the natural function of the woman and burned in their desire toward one another, men with men committing indecent acts and recciving in their own persons the due penalty of their error" (Roman1:24).

2. Homosexuals have become bold even arrogant in demanding society's approval for their indecent acts. Society is accepting and even supporting these sexual immoralities. Teresa Hairston, author of Gospel Today, asks are we spiraling towards a Godless society? Where is America heading? Today's society is becoming

the next Sodom and Gomorrah. Where are the people of God? Wake up! We are in a serious battle and we have to fight against this for the kingdom of heaven suffereth violence, and the violent take it by force (Matthew 11:12 KJV).

"God has given space for repentance" (Revelation 2:21). He has declared that "He will cast them into great tribulation unless they repent. The Body of Christ should not become like Jezebel and not repent, for the great day of his wrath is come; and who shall be able to stand" (Revelation 6:17)?

And unto the faithful overcomers, who keep my works unto the end, to him will I give power over the nations; and he shall rule them with a rod or iron (Revelation 2:26 &27 KJV) "I will give you the morning star" (Revelation 22:16 KJV).

It is possible for the Christians today to lose every reward they had ever earned, by their lives not being what it once was for Christ, so "look to yourselves, this is serious business, and don't be a loser when rewards are distributed (2John 8 KJV). It will be a tragic day to have worked all these years to not receive the reward you had expected to receive. Instead, about-face! Live for Him! Be cautious of any attitude. Heed to the warning.

"He, who has an ear, let him hear what the Spirit says to the churches" (Matthew 11:15).

Source Of Paganism Added To The Church

From Genesis 10 to this present day the bodies of Christ have been corrupted by pagans and they are not even aware of it.

A few source of paganism that were added to the church from (A.D. 607 — A.D. 1965).

Penance - Crawling on hands and knees, causing gashes and blood on their body in an effort to punish themselves, whereas the Scripture teaches, "For it is by grace you have been saved, through faith and this not from yourselves, it is the gift of God not by works, so that no one can boast" (Ephesians 2:8-9 KJV). Darkness, the room is kept in a dark and gloomy state; "But whoever lives by the truth comes into the light" (John 3:21 NIV).

Mystery - Mysterious nature of service in which language (Latin) is spoken and no one could understand or no message was given in a language that's recognized; The seeds that fell on good ground are the people who hear and understand the message (Matthew 13:23 CEV).

Idolatry - Prominently located on every wall idols in representing of Christ; "You shall not make for yourself an idol in the form of everything in heaven above or on the earth beneath or in the waters below" (Exodus 20:4 KJV).

Chanting - During service much chanting is performed by the priest; "When you pray, do not keep on babbling like pagans, for they think they will be heard because of their many words" (Matthew 6:7 NIV).

Mary the Central Figure - a large picture of Mary framed in gold occupies the most prominent place in the cathedral, while the idol representing Christ is off to the left and not nearly so prominent. The Bible teaches "that in everything he (Christ) might have the supremacy" (Colossians 1:18 NIV).

Crucifix - in Roman forms of worship, was all that could be seen of our blessed Lord, where the Scriptures speak not of "continual sacrifice" but, in the words of Christ Himself speaking of the sacrifice, "It is finished"; the angel on the day of resurrection said, "He is not here; he has risen, just as he said" (Matthew 28:6 NIV).

Others examples are as follows:

1 Kissing the Pope's foot
2 Marking and piercing of the body
3 Worshipping of images and relics
4 Easter
5 Use of "holy water" begun
6 Fasting on Fridays and during Lent
7 Christmas
8 Celibacy of the priesthood
9 Prayer beads
10 Halloween
11 Sale of indulgences
12 Doctrine of purgatory decreed
13 Valentine's Day
14 Immaculate conception of Mary
15 Groundhog Day
16 Mary proclaimed Mother of the Church

Many believe these assertions and in some instances appear to be the dispenser of their salvation, which contradicts the scriptures. Notice Jesus' own words in (John 14:6 KJV), "I am the way and the truth and the life. No one comes to the Father except through me."

CHAPTER FIVE
Sardis, The Dead Church
(Revelations 3:1-6 KJV)

S ardis means "remnant" and, indeed, in this letter Jesus appears to be calling a remnant of believers out of a spiritually dead environment and into a renewed relationship with him. It also represents, "escaping ones" or those who "come out." This name of "they escape" was for those who escape the Crusades, Inquisitions, and tyranny of the Roman Catholic Church. This period ended during the infancy of the Reformation and the birth of Protestantism.

Sardis was an important, wealthy and a well-known city. Much of its wealth came from its textile manufacturing, dye industry and its jewelry trade. Most of the city practiced pagan worship, and there were many mystery cults or secret religious societies. The magnificent temple of Artemis, dating from the fourth century BC, was one of its points of interest and still exists as an important ruin.

In relation to Sardis, Christ is introduced as the one that has the seven spirits of God in (vs) one, an apparent allusion to the sevenfold character of the Holy Spirit as resting upon Christ according to the prophecy of Isaiah 11:2-5 KJV. There the Holy Spirit is described thus, "the Spirit of the Lord," "the

Spirit of wisdom and understanding, the spirit of counsel and might, the spirit of knowledge and of the fear of the Lord, God and resting upon Christ, and Christ is also revealed as the One who has the seven stars." This was to make clear that the leaders of the church are responsible to no human representative of Christ and must give account directly to the Lord Himself.

The church of Sardis, an ancient of Lydia; according to some Theologians was the first city said to have been converted by the preaching of the Gospel of John, the first city to fall away from the way of Christianity, the first city to be laid in ruins unlike the other Epistles where Jesus began to command them to take an observation with a reproof.

This Church of Sardis had public success but private failures which resulted in spiritual ruins.

The church of Sardis was a church of works, they were not lazy. Their reputation among men was great based on men's standards; they lived respectable and honorable lives on the outside, but in reality this church was contaminated with the world, hypocrisy, inward decay, spiritual disintegration and dry rot that plagued the church. Its museums were of natural history where animals, lifelike in their natural habitat, were mounted exactly as they lived, but they were dead. The Sardis people in the city were surrounded by a severe form of idolatry from the practice of pagan worship mystery cults and for being a secret religious society. Sardis became the mother of dead orthodoxy. And many hundreds of churches are following Sardis's lead today.

The church of Sardis was a church of sound doctrine, a spiritual church and one that had an effective ministry and testimony for God as many of the body of Christ do today. They appeared to be flourishing, their unity among themselves, their worship service was unmatchable. They seemed to have had it all together. But prophetically, they were pronounced "dead". Dead by God as for their spiritual life and power were concerned. In other words a sleeping church that is practically useless. Why? How does a church die spiritually? There is nothing worse than a dead church! It is like a man dying of thirst in a desert who sees a well far off, only to find upon his arrival the well is dry. Are you dead spiritually? Are you a part of a dead Church?

The searching judgment of Christ as it relates to the church of Sardis in modern churches today was full of activities and speaks of Christ but has little to no power and their spiritual life does not reflect the life of Christ. As it says in the scripture; "every man also to whom God hath given riches and wealth, hath given him power" (Ecclesiastes 5:19a KJV). God also states; "except ye abide in the vine you are lifeless and can bear no fruit, he cuts off every branch that doesn't produce fruit" (John15:1&2 NLT).

There was deadness in their souls and services where no one was getting delivered, healed or set free from the power of hell. Demons were not and still are not being cast out, but instead demons are being medicated and counseled. People were and still are today getting caught up in the hype of what is and where it's going on, but yet leaving the same as they were when they arrived. No substance, no power to deal with issues that they may face from day-to-day, or week-to-week.

Jesus said:

"These people honor me with their lips, but their hearts are far away. Their worship is a farce, for they replace God's commands with their own man-made teachings" (Matthew 15:8&9 NLT).

The letter to the Sardian Church breaths the spirit of death, of appearance without reality, promise without performance, outward show of strength betrayed by want of watchfulness and careless confidence.

According to some theologians this Church's untimely death was a matter of history. In 600 A.D., a papal decree made prayer in any language other than Latin illegal. Next, sermons were only spoken in Latin. Finally, Bibles were written only in Latin. Even worst, all Bibles were confiscated; owning one was a capital offence.

Since only the popes, cardinals, bishops and priests knew what the Scriptures said, they could say whatever served their interests and they did as many do today. Many have bibles in their homes, on their job in many places and except whatever is said not judging or studying the word for accuracy for themselves.

Purgatory was conceived and the sale of indulgences became the remedy. Mary became a goddess and rosary beads became a ritual. Holy water was fabricated and confession to priests was mandated. Kissing the pope's feet was ordered and his words became the equivalent of Divine Scripture.

The spiritual history of this church was to correspond to the political history of the city. Their works were also declared to be imperfect, literally not fulfilled, that is not achieving the full extent of the will of God. Their works were also short, either in motive or in execution, and they were exhorted to fill to the fullest the opportunity of service and testimony.

According to other theologians, the church of Sardis had become spiritual Pharisees. The Pharisee's were a conceited, proud, pompous arrogant and self-righteous people who were proud of themselves and their name. The church of Sardis had become rich, prideful, and self-reliant. It was hopelessly infested with satanic rituals, defiling the name "Christian." They were not known in Sardis for the name of God, they were known in Sardis for their name "ye were alive". When you are more proud of your name or denominational name (I'm Rev. Baptist, I'm Dr. Bishop, I'm Methodist, I'm Apostle, I'm non-denominational, I'm Jehovah Witness and I'm Catholic) than the name of Jesus Christ you are practicing idolatry and God said "you have a name" and you are proud of that name. Sardis was more proud of their past reputation of being alive, but they were dead. Are you a spiritual Pharisee?

In the modern Sardis Church today, rules, laws, doctrines and traditions of men govern them. They are faithful to the building, busy doing stuff and God is not acknowledged. The scripture states; "sacrifice and burnt offering I would not, but a body has thou prepared for me." God is a jealous God he wants our total being he wants to be first and foremost in our lives.

The church of Sardis symbolized the Reformation Era. This Reformation Era was born out of the attempts of Christian clerics reforming the Catholic Church. During this period of history, the church was reformed but not revived. Complacency and a new legislation set in. Some essential doctrines were reclaimed such as the one quoted by Martin Luther (a Roman Church Monk); the just shall live by faith (Roman 1:17 KJV), but the changes did not shake loose the elaborate rituals and human traditions of the church, nor of the church today.

Rituals replace righteousness, ceremony replaced the need for change and conformance to the nature of Christ, confession replaced the need of conversion and being born again. They did good things, but did not do Godly things.

They claimed their prestigious membership, they had many religious activities, they had committees, they had a reputation in the city of being alive, they would go to Church, then come over to the church of what's happening. But through all of that religious calisthenics', their activities did not equate to their spirituality, God said "yet they were dead." They were practically riding off of their past reputation and suffering from neglect and indifference. For example, I remember when anointing was used to in services where anointing was brought the wisdom of God through you. I believe it should still be used today.

The church of Sardis was not what they said they were, Sardis was what God said they were. And so what is God saying about you today? Are you alive, yet dead?

This was a dangerous stage for the church because it included the entire population, thus eliminating the need for personal acceptance of Jesus Christ and an emphasis on the individual's relationship to God, and also the tendency to obey government rather than God. When the scripture clearly reads, "we ought to obey God rather than men" (Acts 5:29 KJV), especially when it goes contrary to the explicit commands of God and so be ready to suffer the consequences of your stand.

God's Counsel

But you are dead…. "Be watchful, and strengthen the things which remain, that are ready to die, for I have not found your works perfect before God. "Awake thou that sleepest…. and Christ shall raise you from the dead" (spiritually speaking). No church is ever killed by outside foes. Why? "Jesus said upon this rock I build my church and the gates of hell shall not prevail against it" (Matthew 16:18 KJV). A church lives based on the individual spiritual hunger of the individual members and a church dies through the spiritual death of its membership. You need to be filled with the Holy Spirit and not just stop at salvation.

You can be a dead church and not know it, as Samson lost his power and didn't know it. The bible "says he knew not that the Lord had departed from him"

(Judges 16:20 KJV). Samson shook himself just to find out the anointing had left.

Many churches today are just shaking themselves as Samson did just to find out that the anointing has departed. When the anointing comes everybody knows it but when it leaves even Samson did not know it. Why? The modern church just goes on with their every day/ Sunday routine or programs, not acknowledging God in who he is.

Don't be that church of today that seems to have had an acceptable name in certain areas but in reality is dead. This is a tragic view of the fact that life is a characteristic of the born-again Christian. Jesus said, "I have come that you may have life, and that more abundantly" (John 10:10 KJV).

God had given his church an empowerment to evangelize the world (Matthew 28:19 KJV), and the biblical characteristic the Body of Believers should be reflecting is being led by the Spirit of God (Roman 8:14 KJV). You cannot chose one aspect of this responsibility and neglect the others.

The main purpose of the church was the propagation of the gospel of Jesus Christ.

When people leave your church with the mystery feeling of "worship" but have not been brought face to face with Jesus Christ in a personal way, they have been worshipping in a dead church. Ritual and formality, characteristic of pagan forms of worship, are not conductive to genuine worship, for they appeal to the sensuous human nature, but the Bible teaches that, "They that worship him must worship him in spirit and in truth (John 4:24 KJV). Ritual that comes from paganism cannot be of the Holy Spirit and does not convey truth.

In the scripture it's noted, "he that hath the Son hath life and he that hath not the Son of God hath not life" (1John 5:12 KJV). The Body of Christ needs to come alive; because we have before us a living gospel, that should motivate us in serving a living Savior and God's expectation of us is to be a living church.

There was an English poem that at one time was a requirement for every student to read. The poem of the Ancient Mariner:

In the poem the corpses of dead men rise to man the ship, they rise to pull the ores, dead men hoist the sail and dead men steer the ship. It all seems impossible, but it's not. As impossible as it seems, those conditions exist in the churches of today.

Dead men are in the pulpit dishonoring the word of God. Preachers of the Gospels are ordaining homosexuals. There are dead men in the pews singing about a Heaven they may not ever see, dead men singing in the choir about a God they don't even know. There are many active house groups, prison ministries, Sunday schools, counseling centers, youth groups, regular intercessory prayer groups and salaried pastor, Spiritual dead!

God said to Sardis and to the church of today, "I know your work" You have a name that said you are alive, but you are dead, dead to the core. And you don't even know it. The works many Believers are doing for God does not necessarily mean its Godly work. Work is trivial.

The Body of Christ can sacrifice all they would like to but if the sacrifices are not acceptable to God they are wasting their time. Read the story of Cain and Abel. Both men labored bringing a sacrifice to God but only Abel's sacrifice met God's standards. Why build a temple if God wants you to build an Ark you will certainly regret it. Why bring vegetables when God wants Lamb you will be disappointed.

Sardis and many churches today have programs that work, but God wants your worship in spirit and in truth. Jesus also states that he found the Christians in Sardis and the churches of today work not perfect before Him (Revelation 3:2b KJV). That incompleteness could be referred to as a number of deeds. Maybe many had a building project, which was not finished. Maybe the promise was to give more time to evangelism, and they went back on what they promised.

Maybe the incompleteness of the works describes the quality of the church member's deeds. The deeds are done but don't measure up to the standard Jesus set. Works acceptable to Christ are love, faithfulness, and perseverance, keeping Christ's words and not denying his name. Are these Christian virtues maturing in your lives? If not then your works are incomplete.

Are you alive?

If not, then you can live; as the Israelites were like dry bones dead, and with no hope of restoration; he said unto me, Prophesy upon these bones; and unto them, O ye dry bones, hear the word of the Lord…….Behold, I will cause breath to enter into you, and ye shall live (Ezekiel 37:4&5b KJV):

Living things reproduce themselves, Christians reproduce themselves, and they are soul winners. Soul winners is not a gift, soul winning is a command. Go and win the lost (Matthew 28:19 KJV), that's not a recommendation, that's a command. Do you have any spiritual children? If you don't have spiritual children then you should be embarrassed. Who is the king of Glory to the believers? If Christ is in the hearts of the believers, the Hope of Glory, and if the believers believe that Heaven is forever and Hell is too long, then why are the believers not sharing that God is the one that's mighty in battle the King of Glory? The Body of Christ should be ashamed.

Living things hunger and thirst (Matthew 5:6 KJV) after righteousness: for they shall be filled. Many have come to the house of the Lord and many have eaten the finest of the finest of food for so long they have become spoiled rotten. And many of the churches today have had a good reputation but a bad Christian testimony and appear beautiful outward, but within were full of dead men's bones (Matthew 23:27 KJV).

But then John writes, "Repent or I will come to you as a thief in the night" (Revelation 3:3 KJV). This repentance is for personal repentance, the entire church, yea, and the entire movement. The Modern churches of today need to turn back to God, seeking His Kingdom, teaching His Gospel rather than giving mans' ideals of what they think is theological truth.

How does that make you feel, knowing that Christ is coming in the clouds of heaven with power and great glory (Matthew24:30 KJV)? Is that something you dread, or is that something that is welcome? Depending on your response, many are either dead or alive.

Believers can belong to a failing local church body and still succeed. Believers belong to a worldly church and still walk properly with Jesus. Every person around the believers can be failing God but someone's faithfulness can still be to God. Leaders may fall into sin but you don't have to fall. Many can be selfish, unforgiving and bitter but you individually don't have to be. The Body of Christ does not have to be spiritually polluted just because everyone else is spiritually polluted.

Don't be a part of the doctrine of Balaam "hypergrace"; as Joe Van Koevering would call it, which is the doctrine that makes no difference on how you live; the grace of God will cover all your sins. Wrong! God's grace will give you time to confess your sins and repent of your sins.

Joe Van Koevering goes on to say, stop preaching someone else's message, preach God's message. Stop your slide. Hold fast! Don't let anything else go. Salvage any good that is still in your modern churches. Remember what was once imparted, once heard and return to what was once received. Stop doing your own thing, and do God's thing. Stop compromising with the world. The day will come that the Body of Believers will answer to God. Will God change many from mortality to immortality (1Corinthians 15:53 KJV)? Will your name be blotted out of the lamb book of life? Make sure YOUR experience is real! For the Lord will confess your name before His father and before his angels (Revelation 3:5b KJV). "He that hath an ear, let him hear what the spirit says to the church" (Matthew 11:15).

CHAPTER SIX
Philadelphia, The Church Christ Loved
(Revelations 3:7-13 KJV)

Philadelphia literally means "brotherly love," and was located in a Greek civilization. This city was plagued with severe earthquakes that nearly destroyed the area around 17 A.D. Tiberius Caesar, the great builder of cities, reestablished it. And according to history this city was founded approximately 189 years before Christ by the king of Pergamos, Attalus II, whose other name was Philadelphus, for which the city was named. This Philadelphia city was the last bastion of Christianity when Islamic Turks overran Asia Minor.

The word "brotherly love" is not associated merely with brothers, but of brotherly love. The word Love is the most used and misunderstood word in the English Language. This word love tumbles out of our mouth habitually, compulsively and not effectively.

Then what does love means?

Love is not an emotion.

What is "brotherly love"?

Brotherly love is not the brotherhood of man. Brotherly love is not humanitarianism. Brotherly love is not a license to sin. Then what is brotherly love? Brotherly love is a Godly love that demands confession of sin, "for God so loved the world that he gave his only begotten Son" (John 3:16 KJV). Brotherly love is tough love. Brotherly love will walk with you through the fault, but will not condone you in the fault. Brotherly love is love that can love the unlovable. Brotherly love is Calvary love. Brotherly love is Agape love. Brotherly love is when Jesus looked down from the cross at the ones who were murdering him and said, "Father forgive them; for they know not what they do" (Luke 23:34 KJV). Brotherly love is Stephen in the Book of Acts, while the people were stoning him to death knelt down and cried with a loud voice, "Lord, do not hold this sin against them" (Acts 7:60 NIV).

Do you know who lead the mob that stoned Stephen? A Pharisee by the name of Saul; God changed his name to Paul and who wrote most of the New Testament.

This is something, when sometimes the people who are hurting you the most become some of the most powerful spiritual leaders, only by you having the grace to bless them instead of cursing them. Many bible scholars believe Paul would have never been heard of if Stephen would have cursed him instead of blessed him.

The bible states, "a new commandment I give unto you, that ye love one another; as I have loved you, that ye also loved one another. By this shall all men know that ye

Seven Churches

are my disciples, if ye have love for one to another" (John 13: 34&35 KJV). This is the love that God expects His people to exemplify. We say the word love so loosely, but is it real? Is this love really being acted out in the hearts of God's people today or are you just going through the motions? A genuine love within the hearts of God's people will have a greater impact on the society of today. Because according to the Word of God it reads; "Yea, I have loved thee with an everlasting love: therefore with loving-kindness have I drawn thee" (Jeremiah 31:3 KJV).

"The harvest is so great, but the workers are so few" (Luke 10:2 NLT)." The passion is not there to win the lost at any cost and the love of many has wax cold" (Matthew 24:12 KJV).

The world does not care what you know until you show that you care. Brotherly love is neither what is said nor what you feel but it is what you do.

If I speak with human eloquence and angelic ecstasy but don't love, I'm nothing but the creaking of a rusty gate, it profiteth you nothing (1Corinthians13:1&3bMessage). _Nothing_ in the Greek means totally worthless. "We know that we have passed from death unto life, because you love the brethren" (1John 3:14 KJV). Love is the proof that you are alive. Brotherly love is a language that the deaf can hear and the blind can see.

The church of Philadelphia was very influential in that area of the ancient world and was marked by vitality for life that spurred them to evangelize, they were a

71

faithful church thus they were called the missionary church.

Philadelphia stood for a well-defined movement in the history of the professing church.

J.N. Darby spoke of the historical churches:

> "Outside of Scripture, the historical church never was, as a system, the institution of God or what God had established, but at all times, from its first appearance in ecclesiastical history, the departure as a system from what God established and nothing else.

> He goes on to say;

> and as to doctrines, it is quite certain that neither a full redemption nor a complete possessed justification by faith, as Paul teaches it, a perfecting forever by Christ's one offering, a known personal acceptance in Christ, is ever found in any ecclesiastical writings after the Scriptures, for centuries.

The church of Philadelphia was the church of the missionaries, the church of the evangelists, the church of the Bible societies, the church of the soul winners, and the church of worldwide preaching of the gospel of the Son of God.

God had a vision!

"Where there is no vision, the people perish" (Proverb 29:18 KJV).

God worked in a thrilling manner that produced revivals which in turn produced what is known today as the modern missionary movement.

Due to the teaching in this movement, it contributed to a consecrated and separated church and increased the zeal for evangelism and missionary sacrifice that fulfilled the Great Commission.

The Spirit of God moved so that an English shoe cobbler, by the name of William Carey became the first foreign missionary and many other young people followed who were touched by the spirit of God. The Lord said "he lay upon his shoulder; so he shall open, and none shall shut; and he shall shut, and none shall open" (Isaiah 22:22 KJV). The door here represented an opportunity for testimony, service and witness. God has opened that same door today. Why has many of the Body of Christ not taking advantage of that opened door?

This church was not spiritually strong, they had been developed outside of the Reformation from the spiritually dead state church but they took advantage of that opportunity and did not make any excuses as many of the people of God do today. One of the church of Philadelphia's strengths was they kept the word of His patience and His name. This is a command for each of us to never deny His name, for if you deny him, he also will deny you" (2Timothy

2:12 KJV). Oh, the tremendous loss some will experience when "we appear before the judgment seat of Christ;" that every one may receive the thing done in his body (2Corinthians 5:10 KJV). While it is true that for the Christians there is "no condemnation" (Roman. 8:1 KJV), it is not correct to assume that God will not hold you responsible for the deeds done in your body.

God's Nature Revealed

1. "HOLY." The Lord reminds of us of His holiness. For such a high priest became us, who is Holy, harmless, undefiled, separate from sinners, and made higher than the heavens; (Hebrews 7:26 KJV) And the Lord said, "Be ye holy; for I am Holy" (1 Peter 1:16 KJV). Holiness is not optional and holiness is not from the things you do. This aspect of His nature signified the practice of the church of Philadelphia in being separated from the world unto holiness. Follow peace with all men, and holiness, without which no man shall see the Lord (Hebrew 12:14).

2. "True." Dr. J. Vernon McGee offers this interesting suggestion: "True means genuine with an added note of

perfection and completeness, Moses did not give the 'true bread.' Christ is the 'true bread" (John 6:32-35 KJV). Jesus said sanctify them through thy truth: thy word is truth (John 17:17 KJV). Christ is not only truth, but also the ultimate truth. And the Word was made flesh, and dwelt among us, (and we beheld his glory, as of the only begotten of the Father,) full of grace and truth (John 1:14 KJV). The Christ of truth and the word of truth are inseparable. No truth will be given to this world other than the truth revealed in Jesus Christ. This aspect of His nature alluded to the movement toward doctrinal separation.

3. "....who holds the key of David" this refers to the authority of Christ, His rulership of the world. The key of David and the open door go together. The key of David means Christ has all authority in heaven and in earth. He has the keys of death, hell, and the grave. He has absolute authority. Jesus said I am the root and the offspring of David and the bright morning star (Revelation 22:16 KJV). He gives latitude to the kings of the world; He

nevertheless controls the extent to
which they can be governed.

4. "What he opens no one can shut, and
what he shuts no one can open." The
Lord Jesus gave His disciples the
commission to "go into the entire
world and preach the good news."
"All authority in heaven and on earth
has been given to me." For a great
door is opened unto me, and therefore
are many adversaries (1Corinthians
16:9 KJV) this door is open for service.
The Lord Jesus Christ controls the
doors of opportunity for preaching the
gospel. The Lord said I am the door:
by me if any man enters in, he shall be
saved, and shall go in and out, and
find pasture. When God opens a door
for you and you step into a new
Spiritual dimension right on the other
side of that spiritual dimension is a
fresh anointing but there is also a
fierce battle because the prince of
darkness is not going to allow you to
take people out of the kingdom of
darkness and put them in the
kingdom of light without a battle. No
one, not one world dictator can close
the door to the preaching of the
Gospel unless Christ so wills it.

There is a tendency to compromise in order to gain opportunities, whereas in truth it is our responsibility to do right, because God is not limited in His ability to open doors, God is responsible for opening the doors of opportunity. In Isaiah 22:20-22 KJV the Bible states the characterization of Eliakim, the steward of King Hezekiah. This noble, trusted man was given the key to the palace. No one came to approach the king except through Elikim. So it is with us in Christ.

God's Commendation

I know thy works: behold, I have set before thee an open door, and no man can shut it: for thou hast a little strength, and hast kept my word, and hast not denied my name.

This evidently refers to the door of opportunity open to them for the proclamation of the gospel, one of the chief characteristics of faithful service throughout this Church age.

Of course, the real strength for us as the believers is the Holy Spirit. For Paul writes "my grace is sufficient for thee: for my strength is made perfect in weakness" (2Corinthians12:10 KJV). Just because you may be classified as a small group does not mean you are a weak group, as it was for the Philadelphia Church Age. They gained strength through unity; "For where two or three are gathered together in my name, there am I in the midst of them" (Matthew 18:20 KJV).

Today, the Word of God is in special question everywhere. Many modern world organizations and philosophers try to lower and take away the authority of this world. The voice of the church (clergy) is substituted for Christ's voice. Religion is an earth born thing-not heaven born, an aspiration, but not an inspiration. But we can be just like the Philadelphians, and not only believe the Word of God, but also exemplify a spirit of true obedience of the Word of God. There were reasons for names. Satan is the liar from the beginning always trying to counteract lies to destroy the power of the truth and the effective work of God.

When God took the special name of Jehovah with Israel, it meant that He was going to approve Himself to them in that character, as the immutable God, the "I AM" upon whom, they could rely to keep the covenant. So in order for prophecy to be fulfilled Christ Immanuel, "God is with us" He was called 'Jesus,' His people's Savior from their sins. God could not be with us without our sins being met and none but a divine person could meet them, salvation must be of God, and this is all expressed in that name "Jesus."

Christ in the Greek form of the Hebrew "Messiah" speaks of Him as the anointed of God to be the deliverer, a Prophet to bring out of error, a priest to open the way to God, and a king to govern for God.

To confess His name involves the confession: of His absolute deity, His true humanity, His salvation of His people, and His being their only and sufficient Teacher, Intercessor and Lord. The name of Christ expresses what He is. The truth of what He is, is what is committed to us, what we have to confess in the face of the world.

God's Advice

Why are many churches of today having a hard time maintaining the status quo—as they are losing more members than they are taken in. Could this be because they have not "kept his word" and or because they have "denied his name?" For whatever the reason is the body of believers needs to go back to the basics.

The Bishop Dr. Walter Thomas of (New Psalmist Church Baltimore, Maryland) states on 9 January 05 The Word Network, there are essential elements needed to build and maintain a spiritual ministry: evangelism, missions, and the revelation of the Word of God.

Nothing ignites the fire of evangelism in the heart of God's people like a dynamic message on the promised return of Jesus.

He goes on to say;

> many have gotten caught up in church work that they have forgotten the mission: The mission to prepare men and women on

how to live for God, through the Word of God. The Body of Christ needs God to teach us as ambassadors of God (Mentorship); because mentorship will birth out discipleship.

The body of believers should have someone they can mimic when it comes to spirituality. Spirituality is not prosperity, materialism, wealth in money, cars, and homes, but it's a relationship with God that brings prosperity.

If an individual believes some of the Word of God but not all the Word of God they are not considered good examples of the Word of God.

The people of the world are philosophically empty and aware of that emptiness because the church of today is not emulating the life, vitality and the power of the Spirit of God within them. Those that are faithful churches with bible teaching, evangelistic, missionary, minded needs to lead people of this world out of their philosophical desert and into the abundant life Christ came to offer all humankind.

Awake! "I am coming soon." Hold on to what you have already been doing or get what you had not done and to continue faithfully until the end, so that no one will take your crown.

God's Promises

Christ promises that He will vindicate. "He will make heretics, those who were the synagogue of Satan, who claim to be Jews though they were not, but were liars—he will make them come and fall down at your feet and acknowledge that I have loved you." Do you know that the saints shall judge the world? (1Corinthians 6:2 KJV). Christ promised that all the false religionists (religious impostors and false teacher) who claimed to be Jew, but were not, would someday be subdued before them. Christ himself spoke of that time when He stated: "As I live, saith the Lord, every knee shall bow to Him, and every tongue shall confess to God" (Roman 14:11 KJV).

He promises that the church will be spared from the day of the Lord's wrath, or the horror of the Tribulation period. "Since we have kept His command to endure patiently, He will preserve us; also keep us from the hour of trial that is going to come upon the whole world to test those who live on the earth." The teachings of Jesus and the writings of Paul clearly teach that the true Church will be caught up before the Tribulation Period begins.

We the believers are not earth dwellers, for "this world is not our home; we are only passing through;" For our citizenship is in heaven (Philippians 3:20 KJV). We are exercising a tremendous amount of faith to prepare for Jesus' coming.

Paul says, for if we would judge ourselves, we would not be judged (1Corinthians11:31 KJV). The standard we will use to judge ourselves is God's Word: For the word of God is living and powerful, and sharper than any two-edged sword......and is a discerner of the thoughts and intents of the heart (Hebrew 4:12 KJV). The word *discerner* is also translated "judge"." The Word of God is the judge of the intent of each and every one of our hearts.

The Apostle Peter says, "the time has come for judgment to begin at the house of God" (1Peter 4:17 KJV). Our just God is judging us, His children, by having us judge ourselves daily with the Word. God has a perfect plan for us. And if we abide by it, we will see the desired results reflected in our lives.

"Thus said the Lord, Stand ye in the ways, and see, and ask for the old paths, where is the good way, and walk therein, and ye shall find rest for your souls" (Jeremiah 6:16 NKJ).

Can what we go through (tribulation) be designed for our (saints) perfection? Asked a new convert;

No, it will violate the teaching of the Apostle Paul; where Paul states, and He Himself (Jesus) gave some (the Church), to be apostle, some prophets, some evangelists, and some pastors and teachers, for the equipping (perfecting) of the saints for the work of ministry (Ephesians 4:11,12 KJV). Paul says it's the ministry that perfects us (the Saints), not the tribulation.

Paul also reveals that the Lord will present to Himself a glorious church, not having spot or wrinkle or such thing, but that we the body of believers should be holy and without blemish (Ephesians 5:27 KJV).

We will see that it will be by ministry that we the church will become glorious, spiritually mature and ready to be caught up to meet the Lord in the air. No amount of tribulation or persecution could produce such an accomplishment. "He also promises to return for His own, and He promises rewards for us the (Saints) who overcome.

This clearly identifies us the believers as God's own possessions and the inhabitants of the New Jerusalem. We will be as pillars in the temple of God, and He will write on us His new name!

"And I will write upon them my new name." and " my name shall be called Wonderful, Counselor, the Mighty God, the Everlasting Father, the Prince of Peace" (Isaiah 9:6 KJV). Our new name will identify us and allow us access into the Holy City of God. It also will entitle us to be His servants, where we shall see His face (Revelation 22:3-4 KJV).

This is one of the blessed promises in the Word of God to us His children that one day we will see the One who is the object of our affection, the Lord Jesus Christ, whom we have worshipped in spirit and in truth through the Word of God. That is, we will see Him face–to-face.

"He that hath an ear, let him hear what the Spirit saith unto the churches" (Matthew 11:15).

CHAPTER SEVEN
The Church of Laodicea
(Revelation 3:14-22 KJV)

Laodicea from the Greek word laos means (people) and dika meaning (the rights or requirements), Laodicea is the "judging or rights of people," or the voice of the people demanding their absolute rights. This is taking place right now. The voices of the people are trying to overrule the Word of God. This is the time where everything is established order; the law of the land and the righteous Word of God will bow to the will of the people.

The Laodicea church is a church with the spirit of anarchy. The spirit of anarchy is when men are doing that which is right in their own eyes. Also the spirit of anarchy says my thoughts are as good as the thoughts of the Word of God. We see this taking place right now as with mainline churches ordaining practicing homosexuals. God said that, lifestyle is an abomination, yet many churches are putting their hands on it and saying this is of God. Now who is right, the Word of God or the will of the people?

The Church of Laodicea and many of the churches today have watched the moral freefall of America in absolute silent.

So what was so wrong with this church and many churches of today? Why does God so harshly condemn them?

They had works. But their works were rendered in a lukewarm fashion; meaning they were not "hot," "zealous of good works," nor were they "cold," and lifeless.

The Holy Spirit warns that a lukewarm church, which claims to represent Jesus Christ, never sees transformation of a soul from darkness to life, but instead deceives many because they do not have the power of the gospel of Christ. These churches are usually more interested in social action than gospel action, more interested in reformation than transformation, more interested in planning than praying. And the Lord Jesus Christ does not claim them even though they make their claim on Him.

Laodicea Message

The church of Laodicea became famous all because of their wealth, their bankers, their medical school, their popular eye salve, and their textile industry. They arrogantly said, I am rich, I have become wealthy, and I have no need for anything.

They are deceived about themselves! And their most devastating deception is self-deception.

This can be dressed up anyway the People of God would want too dress it.

This message to the church of Laodicea and the churches of today was a bold, blunt, brutal, repudiation message. Christ says, spiritually the Believers of the church were poor, blind, and naked, wretched and pitiful. True wealth is found only in God's grace. That the trial of your faith, being much more precious than gold that perisheth, though it be tried with fire, might be found unto praise and honor and glory at the appearing of Jesus Christ (1Peter1:7 KJV). You have no spiritual value gold, virtue, white raiment, undoubtedly, the "garment of salvation" and the "robe of righteousness" or vision, eye salve. I will spew you out of my mouth, which literally translate in Greek to "I will vomit you out of my mouth" that means you are disgusting to me.

Why does God hate luke warmness? Luke warm robs the people of God from reaching their potential. No champion athlete ever plays a game half-heartedly, they always play their best. No champion for Christ should ever allow a corrupt society to destroy their divine destiny or to control their spiritual potential.

Lukewarm is a total misrepresentation of Jesus Christ as a person. Jesus was intense, Jesus was passionate and Jesus was also revealed in Revelation as Jesus with fire in his eyes and out of his mouth goeth a sharp sword, that with it he should smite the nations: and he shall rule them with a rod of iron.........That shall cast them into the furnace of fire, there shall be wailing and gnashing of teeth (Matthew 13:50 KJV).

Laodicea Description

This Luke warm condition was considered an emetic when one has swallowed poison in order to make them regurgitate. A lukewarm church is emetic to Christ.

If people would look at the Church of Laodicea and many churches of today, It will show the churches as being a church of great wealth, a church full of well-to-do members, a parking lot full of luxury cars, stained glass, a robed choir, and a cultured limp wrist preacher. That is all good as long as Christ is the one who's being Glorified in all it.

This material abundance is not conducive to spiritual vitality. The church of the finest and fabulous architecture, million-dollar buildings, fund-raising organizations, and even a large, though unconsecrated church membership. In saying, "The Church has acquired wealth and does not need a thing," does the Church not realize your poverty-stricken spiritual state? For Jesus said, "Apart from me you can do nothing."

Human beings can organize, build, promote, preach, and even teach, but only the Spirit of God can convict human souls. Only the Spirit of God can transform the lives of people. Christ is the refiner of the human soul, which he purifies as the refiners do gold (Malachi 3:3). Only the Spirit of God can glorify Jesus Christ, who said of the Holy Spirit, "He will bring glory to me" (John 16:14 KJV). If it glorifies humanity, it is not the work of the Spirit!

To Christ he sees:

1. "Wretched, pitiful."- in all the lessons on positive thinking and books read on how to find peace, inwardly the people are still unhappy, wretched lot, for riches and the human hungry hearts can never be satisfied. They spend forty years accumulating their

wealth and the final thirty years keeping others from getting it.

2. "Poor." Even though rich in material things people of God are poor because they do not know Him. This is in accord with the Word of God; what good would it do to get everything you want and lose you, the real you" (Mark 8:36 message)?

3. "Blind." Many think they know and understand through their sophisticated education and appropriation of "wisdom," but they do not understand the ways of God. The body of Christ is in need of spiritual illumination. No matter how brilliant people are in the flesh, unless the Spirit of Jesus Christ dwells in them, they will never understand the ways of God. For the natural man receiveth not the things of the Spirit of God (1Corinthians 2:14a KJV). The pulpits of churches are being used today as sounding boards for example segregation agitation (color, religion, women, status and etc.) and other reasons, which depicts the blindness of churches because they are striving to solve these problems externally.

That's impossible! Because these problems can only be resolved internally through Jesus Christ! They don't see the need of the millions who are dying without the Savior and going into eternal loss.

4. "Naked." The churches are clothes with religion, and not clothes by faith with garments of righteousness. Nakedness symbolized spiritual shame and worthlessness (2 Corinthians 5:3 KJV). For he hath made him to be sin for us, who knew no sin; that we might be made the righteousness of God in him (2 Corinthians 5:21 KJV). They have excluded the divine Son of God from their midst but without Him they are nothing.

Laodicea Counsel

In the book of the prophet Isaiah (55:1 KJV), it reads God's invitation to human beings to come and buy what they need "without money and without cost." Salvation is not purchased through human efforts. It has been purchased for us by the death of Jesus Christ on Calvary's cross. Therefore, the poorest of the poor can pay the price, which is to humble oneself, calling on the name of the Lord and believing in him.

"Here I am! I stand at the door and knock: If anyone hears my voice and opens the door, I will come in and eat with him, and he with me" (Revelation 3:20 KJV). This door is referred to as the door of ones heart, that is, the center of one's being. The Bible says, "Above all else, guard your heart, for it is the wellspring of life" (Proverb 4:23 KJV).

Consequently, we find Christ knocking at the door of our emotional center called the heart, asking entrance. He's not forcing his way in, but patiently knocks: How does He knock?

1. Through His Word. The Lord Jesus said, "I tell you the truth, whoever hears my word and believes him who sent me has eternal life and will not be condemned; he has crossed over from death to life" (John 5:24 KJV). Many have felt the gentle knock of their heart and even hear the Word of God, and the knocking evidences itself by violent reaction and rejection, but that does not minimize the fact that Christ has knocked.

2. Through His people. The scripture says, "And how can they hear without someone preaching to them" (Roman 10:14 NIV)? Dr. Lee Scarborough told a story about an encounter he had with a well-to-do businessman who came forward at the close of a service

of prayer; He asked who God used to speak to him about Christ? D. L. Moody, George Truette; He replied: None of those great preachers (D.L. Moody, George Truette, etc) moved me. About eight years ago God saved my wife. I have watched her now these last years, as she has been faithful to Jesus Christ in poverty and in riches. Night after night I've watched her kneel beside our bed to pray. I've watched her as she went faithfully to prayer meetings and church services, putting Jesus Christ first in every area of her life. Last night as we retired, when she kneeled to pray, I began to think of the difference between her life and mine. As I lay there, I thought of my life as a little molehill of nothing and her life as a great mountain for God and righteousness. I got up out of bed and for the first time in eight years asked her to pray for my soul. Last night, by my bedside, I was lead to Jesus Christ—not by D. L. Moody or George Truett, but by my wife. Yes, God knocks on humans' hearts through His people.

3. Through His Holy Spirit. The Lord Jesus made it clear in (John 14:8 KJV)

that He sent the Holy Spirit to convict the heart of humankind of "sin and righteousness and judgment." Many who think they have escaped the preacher and the Word of God have been awakened in the middle of the night to toss restlessly on their bed at the conviction of God's Spirit, which is the gentle knocking of Jesus at the door of one's heart.

4. Through Providence. God's gentle alignment of the affairs of a person's life that continually points him or her to the need of inviting Jesus into your heart. Many who felt the hot breath of death on them recognize that they were saved by the providence of God.

This is a true story about a family in Texas:

Yesterday I closed my store early and went for a ride with my family. We were crossing the railroad tracks when a train struck the back of our car. We were all frightened when we got home. There was only one member of our family, little Mary, saved and a member of a church, who was not frightened. We talked about it and Mary said, "Daddy, if we would have been one second later in crossing that track all the family would have been in hell now except me." As soon as Mary said that, I called my family together for prayer and asked Mary to lead us to Jesus.

Have you accepted His promise?

Hebrew 12:6 KJV comes to mind: "For whom the Lord loveth he chasteneth, and scourgeth every son whom he receiveth." Spirtual spankings are administered in order that we might be zealous and repent, or "change our minds."

Laodicea Challenge

The challenge of Christ to Laodicea and the church of today is to "overcome" or to become "born-again believers." The challenge is simple, a promise to share His throne as He shares the Father's throne. This is a promise that the ones that endure will rule and reign with Christ in His coming kingdom. The ultimate victory of the Christian, not seen in this life but in the life to come, is a challenge to faithfulness. Are the born-Again Believers listening to what our Lord has said to the churches? The message of Christ to Laodicea and the society of today indicate as this age draws to a close, apostasy, deadness, and indifference will increase. No wonder the Lord our God asked; however, when the son of man comes, will he find faith on the earth?'" (Luke 18:8 NAS)

It is time for the church of today to admit where they are spiritually and face the facts to why they are in that state and what they can do to get back on the right standing with God.

The bible states; nothing is impossible to those who believe; it also says; we can do all things through Christ who strengthens us,

Someone who is red-hot for the Lord walks with Him and is sensitive to Him. Even if they make a mistake, they are close enough to God to receive instruction and help for correction. They steadily progress forward. Someone who is cold is usually honest enough to admit they are out of fellowship with God and don't want a relationship right now, but a Luke-warm individual gives off an impression that they have it all together but in reality they are trying to manipulate their way through the system.

Don't be manipulative or intimidate by halfhearted or Luke warm people who want to be in control. They will attempt to convince many they have a close relationship with God and justify their lack of spirituality. Take charge of your life or someone else will.

People can be unreasonable, people can be illogical and self-centered, but love them anyway. If the Saints of God do well, people will accuse the Saints of being selfish or having ulterior motives, but do well anyway. If Christians are successful they will gain false friends and true enemies, but be successful anyway. Honesty and frankness will make the Body of Christ vulnerable, but be honest and frank anyway.

The people of God need to give the Lord the best they have, they will be criticized by someone; Jesus was. It is crucial that the body be ready at all times for those individuals who may be ready to receive the Savior before He returns for His church.

This disturbing indictment against the church of Laodicea echoes a wake-up call to Christians today. Finally, one last time, the Lord proclaims the warning..........Christ invites us to hear His voice. He promises to come in and commune with us.

"He that hath an ear, let him hear what the Spirit saith unto the churches" (Matthew 11:15).

CHAPTER EIGHT
Christ's Description Of Himself

For I am the Lord, I change not; (Malachi 3:6 KJV).

"I am the Alpha and the Omega."

"I am the First and the Last." This speaks of Christ's eternity.

"I am the Living One; I was dead…….." This indicates His life on the earth and His crucifixion.

"I am alive for ever and ever!" This speaks of His resurrection and eternity.

"And I hold the keys of death and Hell." Christ controls who goes to hell and the future of all believers.

"These are the words of him who holds the seven stars in his right hand." Christ controls the messengers of the churches.

"…….and walks among the seven golden lampstands." Christ walks among the churches, easily accessible to them if they desire.

"These are the words of him who is the First and the Last, who died and came to life again." Here Christ combines a reference to His eternal nature with the fact of

His death and resurrection. "These are the words of him who has the sharp, double-edged sword." Christ presents the Word of God as His offensive to weapon.

"...the Son of God." This asserts Christ's relationship to God as His divine Son.

"....whose eyes are like blazing fire." This is an obvious reference to His searching gaze on the work of His Church.

"...whose feet are like burnished bronze?" Bronze, or brass, speaks of judgment. The Lord Jesus Christ will one day judge all people.

"These are the word of him who holds the seven spirits of God and the seven stars." The Holy Spirit will guide the "star" messengers of the churches. The Church has never been without guidance, if she would look for it.

"These are the words of him who is holy." His nature is holy.

"...and true." His testimony is right and can be relied upon.

"...who holds the key of David?" Authority to rule over God's people is His.

"What he opens no one can shut, and what he shuts no one can open." Christ controls our opportunities to serve Him.

"These are the words of the Amen." He has final authority."...the faithful and true witness." He is the revelation of God.

"...the ruler or (beginner) of God's creation." Christ is the author and source of all God's creation.

"Here I am! I stand at the door and knock. If anyone hears my voice and opens the door, I will come in and eat with him, and he with me." The Lord of glory pictures Himself standing without, knocking at the door of a person's heart. He does not force His entrance, but leaves it to the individual to invite Him to come in.

ARE All Scripture Profitable

Some theologians teach that only the letter to the Laodicea church holds a message for us today. The apostle Paul taught, All Scripture is given by inspiration of God (Every Scripture is God-breathed), and is profitable...(2Timothy 3:16 KJV).

For doctrine, for reproof, for correction, and for instruction are a few areas in which we know Scriptures are profitable. We all especially need instruction in righteousness, which is the right standing with God.

Translations produced by modern theologians reduce God's Word to being just another book with no chance of changing a person's life: "For I am not ashamed of the gospel of Christ, for it is the power of God to Salvation" (Roman 1:16 KJV).

All seven letters to the churches are vitally important to us in today's society, because they are the inspired Word of God. Each contains a message for us, either instructions or warnings for us to heed, for if we are falling in those same snares we have an opportunity to be zealous and repent before it's too late.

A Description Of Salvation By Christ Himself

The doctrine of salvation is the most important subject in the Bible next to the person of Christ.

A born again, committed relationship with God is the key to a victorious life. Jesus, the Son of God laid down His life and rose again so we could spend eternity with Him in heaven and experience His absolute best on earth.

Jesus has given salvation, healing and countless benefits to all who call upon His name. These benefits can be yours if you would be zealous, repent and receive Him unto your heart.

The Bible makes it perfectly clear that salvation is a matter of the will, whoever wishes may come.

"To him who overcomes, I will give the right to eat from the tree of life, which is in the paradise of God." Believers will live forever in God's paradise. This is suggestive of an eternal existence comparable to the Garden of Eden: no death, no sin, no heartache, nothing but the blessing of God (Revelation 2:7 KJV).

"He who overcomes will not be hurt at all by the second death." Believers will not be "thrown into the lake of fire" (Revelation 20:15 KJV) "but are saved from eternal death, which means eternal separation from God"

(Revelation 2:11 KJV). "To him who overcomes, I will give...a white stone with a new name written on it, known only to him who receives it." The stone indicates acquittal from our sins, and our new name, just as Christ renamed Peter and Paul after their conversions, points to the new life we have in Him (Revelation 2:17 KJV).

"To him who overcomes and does my will to the end, I will give authority over the nations. 'He will rule them with an iron scepter; he will dash them to pieces like potter', just as I have received authority from my Father." This indicates believers will rule and reign with Christ in the Millennium (Revelation 2:26-27 KJV).

"I will also give him the morning star." This is Christ's promise to come into the believer's heart and dwell with him or her (Revelation 2:28 KJV).

"He who overcomes will, like them, is dressed in white." The believer's sinful nature is covered by the righteousness of Christ (Revelation 3:5 KJV).

"I will never blot out his name from the book of life." Only those whose names are not written in the Book of Life are "thrown into the lake of fire." Believers need never fear hell, for Christ will see that our names remain in His Book of Life (Revelation3:5 KJV).

"Him who overcomes I will make a pillar in the temple of my God. Never again will he leave it." Believers will have access to the Holy Place of God (Revelation 3:12 KJV) "I will also write on him my new name." Believers will be eternally identified with Christ (Revelation 3:12 KJV).

"To him who overcomes, I will give the right to sit with me on my throne." Believers will have a share in the ruling of Christ's coming kingdom (Revelation 3:21 KJV).

We can appreciate the attitude of the late Dr. Joseph A. Siess, who wrote in his book: The Apoclypse

1. With an honest and ever, prayerful heart, and with these solemn and awful warnings ever before my eyes, I have endeavored to ascertain and indicate in these lectures what our gracious Lord and Master has been so particular to make known and defend. If feebleness, or rashness, or overweening confidence in my own understanding has distorted anything, I can only deplore the fault, and pray God that if I err, God forgive me! If I am right, God bless my feeble testimony! In either case, God speed His everlasting truth!

"He that has an ear, let him hear what the Spirit saith unto the churches" (Matthew 11:15).

EPILOGUE

This book is written with the perspective that we as a nation, a church, a Body of Christ, as Christians and as Born-again believers would stop and take a spiritual physical examination in order to determine if we are falling into any of the areas, the letters God had inspired John to write to the Angels of the Seven Churches of Asia Minor.

For the consistent pattern in the Word of God is that we worship God only and love unconditionally.

"Behold, I am coming soon," This saying does not refer to an appointed time soon to come but means that My coming will take place suddenly and without warning.

Yea, the stock in the heaven knoweth her appointed times; and the turtle and the crane and the swallow observe the time of their coming, but my people know not the judgment of the Lord (Jeremiah 8:7 KJV).

"Blessed is he who keeps the word;" "Happy are those" who are sufficiently aware and ready when that Day arrives. Every individual wants happiness. And the way to eternal happiness is to receive Christ as Lord and

Savior, or to insure our right standing with God, which entitles us an entrance into the Holy City, access to the Tree of Life, and the marvelous blessing of a loving God. The reward of the Lord is with Him, and He will give to everyone according to what they have done.

It's time to hear the word of Christ; and not copy the behavior and customs of this world, but let God transform you into a new person by changing the way you think. Repent and return to zealous following of the Word of God. This Bible is and will always be the truth, no matter how the people of the world and many churches of today devalue it.

The Lord said; my sheep hear my voice and a stranger they will not follow. There are many voices in the world today that want to lure the church to sleep. But it's time to wake up the sleeping giant and silence every voice that's contrary to the will of the Father.

Pastor James Parker quoted in his message; "It's time to get your money working for you;" we need to change currency. The money we have in America is not of value in other countries. Paraphrasing that statement; we need a spiritual overhaul, the work you are presenting to God through darkness is of no value to God if you have not made a kingdom exchange. For Paul wrote: How can light live with darkness (2 Corinthians. 6:14b NLT)?

As the Body of Christ we must always remember as Christians we are forever under the watchful eye of our creator. He sees everything; the word of the Lord says he dwells in the gross darkness which means darkness limits the natural eyes of men but not the supernatural eyes of

God. Which brings to mind, David said "whither shall I go from thy spirit or whither shall I flee from thy presence thou art there" (Psalm 139:7-12 KJV).

None of us is good enough for heaven. But because of God's love for us, Jesus paid the penalty and accepted total punishment for all our offenses against Him, thereby making heaven available to us. Don't be foolish enough to pass up a free ticket to heaven reserving for yourself; a spot in hell.

In the archives of the Supreme Court of the United States is the record of a very strange incident that took place during the term of President Andrew Jackson.

A man named George Wilson who was sentenced to die by hanging for a crime he had committed. Somehow the story came before the president, who granted Wilson a pardon. To everyone's amazement, Wilson tore the pardon to shred and threw it on the floor of his prison cell. The ensuing legal argument concerned the validity of a pardon that was refused, and the question arose as to whether or not Wilson should be freed or hanged. After great deliberation, the U.S. Supreme Court ruled as follows: "A pardon is writing, the value of which is dependent upon the acceptance by the individual for whom it is intended." It was therefore decreed by the court that George Wilson be hanged until dead—not because a pardon was not offered, but because it was not accepted.

This is a perfect picture of those who refuse to take heed of the Word of God, knowing that God has written a pardon for you yet you reject His warnings and thus forfeit your rights to the pardon.

Let the wicked forsake his way, and the unrighteous man his thoughts: and let him return unto the Lord, and he will have mercy upon him; and to our God, for he will abundantly pardon (Isaiah 55:7 KJV).

The verdict is not in the hands of God, it is in the hands of each and every individual and each and every individual are the ones who could determine the outcome of their sentence.

Most assuredly, He says to us, he who hears His words and believes in Him who sent Him has everlasting life, and shall not come into judgment, but has passed from death into life (John 5:24 KJV).

The night is almost gone; the day of salvation will soon be here. So don't live in darkness. Get rid of your evil deeds. Shed them like dirty clothes. Clothe yourself with the armor of right living, as those who live in the light (Roman 13:12 NLT). There is no time for complacency, lethargy and spiritual dullness, no time to become spiritual carcasses. Jesus told the disciples and he's telling the people of God today stay awake, alert and pray. Can the people of God set aside their agenda's and find time to attend their watch? Nehemiah the Prophet said I would stand upon my watch and see what he shall say unto me. The Body of Christ needs to remember what has been imparted into our spirits.

Make that right choice today! "Lift up your heads, because your redemption draws near" (Luke 21:28 KJV), and repent and return zealous to the Word of God.

"Incline your ear, and come unto me: hear, and your soul shall live; and I will make an everlasting covenant with you" (Isaiah 55:3 KJV). It is important that the Body of Christ recognizes the Lords voice and have an ear to what the Lord is saying in these hours.

"He that hath an ear, let him hear what the Spirit saith unto the churches" (Matthew 11:15).

REFERENCES

Loraine Boettner, Roman Catholicism • (Philadelphia: Presbyterians and Reformed, 1962), p.8.

Harry A. Ironside, Lectures on the Book of • Revelation, 12th ed. (Neptune, N.J.: Loizeaux Brothers, 1942).

Quote from White, Paula•

McGee, Dr. J. Vernon•

Harry A. Ironside, Lectures on the book of • Revelation, 12th ed. (Neptune, N.J.: Loizeaux Brothers, 1942), pp.80-81.

Quoted in William R. Newell, The Book of the • Revelation (Chicago: Moody, 1935), p.374.

Henry M. Morris, The Revelation Record: A • Scientific and Devotional Commentary on the Book of Revelation (Wheton, Ill.: Tyndale, 1983), p. 87.

Quote from Parker, Pastor James•

Darby, J. N.•

Ironside, Lectures on the Book of Revelation•

J. Vernon McGee, Reveling Through • Revelation (Los Angeles: Thru the Bible Books Foundation, 1962), 1:82

Lehman Struss, The Book of Revelation • (Neptune, N.J.: Loizeaux Brothers, 1964), p.228.

David L. Cooper, "An Exposition of the Book of • Revelation: The Great Parenthesis (11:15-15:8)," Biblical Research Monthly, 20 (May 1954): p.84.

Clarence Larkin, The Book of Revelation • (Philadelphia: Rev Clarence Larkin Estate, 1919).

Morgan, G. Campbell•

Ironside, Lectures on the Book of Revelation, • pp.81-83.

Phillip Scaff, History of the Christian Church, • vol. 2, pp.750-

H. Grattan Guinness, History Unveiling • Prophecy, pp 41-46, as quoted by Roy From in The Prophetic Faith of our Father (Washington, D.C.: Review and Herald, 1950), p.337.

Boettner, Roman Catholicism, pp. 8-9.•

DeHaan, Dr. M.R. Bible Teacher•

Quote from Martin Teresa Dr.•

Hairston, Teresa, Gospel Today•

McGee, Reveling Through Revelation 2:2.•

Henry H. Halley, Halley's Bible Handbook, 24• th ed. (Grand Rapids: Zondervan, 1965), p.758

Ironside, Lectures on the book of Revelation, • pp. 203-4.

McGee, Reveling Through Revelation, 2:542-43. •

Joseph A. Seiss, The Apocalypse (Grand • Rapids: Zondervan, 1957), p.318.

Gary G. Cohen, Understanding Revelation • (Chicago: Moody, 1978), pp.53-54

Grant Jeffrey, Apocalypse (Frontier Research • Publication, 1992) pp. 85-94s Robert, Oral and Kenneth Copeland

BIBLIOGRAPHY

_____." An Exposition of the Book of Revelation: The Pouring Out of the Bowls of God's Wrath (16:1-21)." Biblical Research Monthly, 19 (October 1954), 186-87

_____. *Dispensational Truth*. Philadelphia: Rev. Clarence Larkin, 1920.

_____. *The Book of Revelation*. Philadelphia: Rev. Clarence Larkin

Boettner, Loraine. Roman Catholicism. Philadelphia:

Bradbury, John W., ed. *Hastening the Day of God*. Wheaton, Ill.: Van Kampen, 1953.

Carl Baugh, "Creation in the Twenty-first Century" television program, Trinity Broadcasting Network.

Chafer, Lewis Sperry, *Systematic Theology*

Church, Jerry R., "Prophecy in the News," Computer Digest

Cooper, David L. "An Exposition of the book of Revelation: The Great Parenthesis (11:15-15:8)." *Biblical Research Monthly*, 19 (May 1954): 84-85,89.

de Liguori, Alphonse, "The Glories of Mary," *Europe* magazine

DeHaan, M.R. *Revelation: 35 Simple studies on the Major Themes in Revelation*. Grand Ripids: Zondervan, 1946.

Drosnin, Michael. The Bible Code. New York: Simon Schuster, 1997.

Edge of Eternity. Coeur d'Alene, ID: Koinonia House, 1999.

French, Nancy, *Computer World* magazine

Gaebelein, A. C., *The Revelation*

Gibbons, Edward, *The History of the Rise and Fall of the Roman Empire*

Grant, F. W. The Revelation of Christ. New York: Loizeaux Brothers, n.d.

Hagee, John, Cornerstone Ministries

Halley, Henry H. *Halley's Bible Handbook*. 24th ed. Grand Ripids: Zondervan, 1965.

Hilsop, Alexander, *The Two Babylons*

Hoar, William P., *Review of the New*

Ironside, Harry A. *Lectures on the Book of Revelation*. 12th ed. New Jersey: Loizeaux Brothers, 1942.

Jeffrey, Grant. *The Handwriting of God*. Toronto, Ont.: Frontier Research Publications, 1997

LaHaye, Tim F. *The Beginning of the End*. Wheaton, Ill.: LaHaye, Tim. *Revelation Unveiled*. Grand Rapids, MI:

Larkin, Clarence. *The Beginning of Daniel*. Philadelphia:

Logsdon, S. Franklin, *Is the USA in Prophecy?*

M'ceyne, Robert Murray , The Seven Churches of Asia

McAulfee, Kathleen, *Omni* magazine

McGee, J. Vernon. *Reveling Through Revelation*, 2 parts. Los

Mendlovitz, Saul, *Review of the News*

Missler, Chuch. *Cosmic Codes: Hidden Messages from the*

Newell, William R. *The Book of the Revelation*. Chicago : Moody, 1935

Noah, Joseph. *Future Prospects of the World According to the*

Ottman, Ford C. *The Unfolding of the Ages in the Revelation of St. John*. New York: " Our Hope," 1905

Pentecost, J. Dwight. Things to come. Grand Rapids: Zondervan, 1957.

Peterson, Paul, *Sinister World Computerization.* Presbyterian and Reformed, 1962.

Rambsel, Yacov. *The Genesis Factor; The Amazing Mysteries of the Bible Codes.* Beverly, Hills, CA: Lions Head Publishing, 2000.

Satinover, Jeffrey. *Cracking the Bible Code.* New York: Morrow, 1997

Scofield, C.I., *Scofield Reference Bibles*

Scott, Paul, *Washington News Intelligence Syndicate*

Scott, Walter. *Exposition of the Revelation of Jesus Christ.* 4th ed. London: Pickering and Inglis, n.d.

Seiss, J.A., *The Apocalypse: Lectures on the Book of Revelation,* Grand Rapids: Zondervan, 1957

Zondervan Publishing House, 1999

ABOUT THE AUTHOR

A postle Dr. Stephanie Veronica Purcell-Parker was born in Macon, Ga, to the late Janie Purcell-Shivers. She graduated from Warner Robins High School in 1980. She is a graduate of Pikes Peaks Community College (Colorado Springs CO.) where she received a Bachelor of Arts and Science Degree in Business Administration Management, a graduate of International Overcoming College of Religion, where she received a Master of Arts in Christian Counseling and Doctorate of Ministry in Pastoral Counseling (Summa Cum Laude), and also graduate of Georgia Bible College, (a satellite school) of Minnesota Graduate School of Theology earning a Doctorate of Theology Degree (Cum Laude). She has also served her country for 18 years retiring from the United States Army.

Whenever you listen to her, her wisdom and knowledge of God's Word inspire you to want to know God intimately and live according to His standards. She's a virtuous woman that exemplifies a woman of Excellence, Prestige and Integrity.

Dr. Parker has received innumerable honors and awards. As a business women, she is the founder and co-owner of Shekinah Glory Enterprises, which umbrella many successful businesses ...Salon and Production Co. just to name a few.

Dr. Parker has been united with Pastor James Parker for 30 years and they are the proud parents of five beautiful children, Yualunda (Shawn), La'kilah (Vernon), Shyvonne, Jaymez and Angel, the God-parents of Organdy and LaShonna, and the prideful grandparents of three handsome grandsons Alan, Syrr and Izaac.

www.ingramcontent.com/pod-product-compliance
Lightning Source LLC
Chambersburg PA
CBHW062001040426
42447CB00010B/1854

Baptism¹⁰¹

Baptism¹⁰¹
What the Bible Says About Baptism

Tim Alsup

Gospel Advocate Company
Nashville, Tennessee

Published by Gospel Advocate Co.
1006 Elm Hill Pike, Nashville, TN 37210
www.gospeladvocate.com

ISBN 10: 089225-570-6

ISBN 13: 978-0-89225-570-2

With thanks to Arinne – a wonderful wife,
a wonderful friend and a wonderful mother.

Table of Contents

BEFORE
YOU BEGIN

I have high hopes for you as you use this book – hopes that what you find here will help you as much as it has helped me.

You see, I enjoy writing, but I wrote this book for more than enjoyment; I believe baptism is a topic that everyone should study. Early in my faith, I realized the confusion many Bible believers seemed to have on the subject of baptism. Is it important or not? How did it start? Why do some groups baptize and some don't? From conversations in dorm rooms and locker rooms and living rooms, with friends and family all across the Bible-based religious spectrum, it was obvious that people disagreed about baptism, which to me, quite honestly, was sad. Sincere individuals all over the place are searching for truth, and yet when it comes to baptism, we all seem unable just to let the Bible speak. Too much historical baggage, I guess.

I was blessed to be raised in a family and church that emphasized the Bible as the only guide in matters of faith. I have heard numerous sermons and read several books on baptism. In studies at Christian colleges, I have been required to write several papers on baptism. I don't claim to have all the answers by any means, but throughout those studies it became clear to me that God has given baptism an important place in His plan.

I wanted to pass that truth along, especially to the sincere people in my life who already believed in Christ and the Bible. The scriptures and logic found in this book have been extremely helpful to me in understanding Christian baptism. I hope they will be helpful to you as well.

I tried to write this book so that it would be useful in multiple contexts: in personal reading, in Bible classes, in small group studies and in evangelism. Before we begin, please allow me to present a few opening thoughts to both the teacher and the personal reader.

Using This Book

Whether you are reading this book or teaching from it, I appreciate you for feeling that this study is important. I agree. I believe a study of baptism should be a life-changing event, both for reflections on our own lives and also for the many people we will talk to about baptism in years to come. So many in our religious world seem to dismiss the subject, and we need to be able to show the world what God says about baptism.

Please read with an open mind. Simply reflect biblically on what you read and decide for yourself whether it is scriptural or not. I have tried to teach scripture accurately at every step, but if you find something you think misses the Bible's teaching, I certainly want you to trust God over me, and I ask that you let me know about the possible error so that I can reconsider it. I am searching to please God, just as I assume you are.

To aid teachers who prefer discussion-oriented classes, I have included two sets of questions at the end of each chapter. I feel the first set, "Discussion Questions," will be more beneficial if you ask them before the class has discussed the material relating to the question. So instead of using these questions as a review, you can use them to carry the class along through discussion. For example, instead of giving all the thoughts of Chapter 1 and then waiting until the end of class to ask why it's important to be able to tell others about baptism (question 2), I would recommend asking the question as you come to that point in the chapter. Let the class give some thoughts, and then add your own, including what the book says about the question. In this way, the students wrestle with the idea in their own minds first, and then when you present the thoughts of the chapter, the material is hopefully more meaningful to them.

The second set of questions at the end of each chapter is titled "Personal

Reflection." Answers to these questions are more open-ended and will vary from person to person. They are meant to help with application. Answering these questions will be a bit more personal, but they should provide genuine sharing and inter-class encouragement if they are discussed. One possibility is to ask the class members to write down their own answers. After a few minutes, ask them to share their answers aloud, and be ready to share some of your own. Discussions of this nature are often most appreciated by youth groups and young adults and can be valuable when included as the application part of a Bible study.

If you are reading this book for personal study, you may be tempted to skip over the chapter questions, but I encourage you to at least wrestle with the "Personal Reflection" questions. Think through them, and let them become a private discussion between you and God. Hopefully they will help you reflect more deeply on living out these biblical principles.

One more thing – please hold on to your copy of this book, and if you are teaching and it is financially possibly, please arrange for each student to have his own copy. I envision this book as a lifelong reference guide so that in future conversations about Christianity with friends and family, we can go back and be reminded of the biblical teaching on baptism. Five years after your study, you or one of your students will be involved in a discussion of salvation or baptism with a friend. Wouldn't it be great to be able to return to this book, be reminded of the biblical logic, and then be better equipped in those conversations?

A Final Word

As I said at the beginning, I have high hopes for this study. I have hopes that those of you who engage in it will grow in your Bible knowledge on the important subject of baptism. I have hopes that your increased knowledge of baptism will be spread to those around you in conversations, studies and searches for truth. I have hopes that souls will be saved as they come to better understand the wonderful blessings God offers through baptism. No doubt you share these same hopes as you begin this study for yourself. If one soul is strengthened or saved as a result of this study, our time has been well spent.

Chapter 1

How Important
IS A STUDY OF BAPTISM?

"[B]ut, speaking the truth in love, [we] grow up in all things into Him who is the head – Christ" (Ephesians 4:15).

Chris could feel all three sets of eyes staring at him as his mind raced 100 miles per hour. He noticed that he was gripping his cup a little tighter as he searched for the right words. How had a Tuesday evening coffee trip suddenly turned so stressful? He had been sitting with some friends at the usual table of the local cafe, a weekly tradition they had enjoyed for more than a year. And in many ways, this outing had been just like every other one they had spent together. They had been laughing about last night's TV shows, making fun of each others' favorite sports teams, previewing next weekend's football matchups, and telling their entertaining stories from the past week. But then something unique had happened. Somehow the conversation had turned to religion. And somehow the focus had turned to Chris.

You see, Chris now worshiped regularly at the Main Street Church of Christ just a few blocks from the cafe, but he had grown up attending the Thompson Road Church of Christ in his hometown. During his sophomore year in high school, he had privately asked his youth minister some questions about heaven and salvation. After looking at a few Bible passages together and having a talk with his parents, Chris made up his mind: He was baptized the next night. Now, years later, right here on an otherwise ordinary Tuesday evening, Chris was asked why he had decided to be baptized. Before he even had a chance to answer, one of his friends expressed his feeling that Chris had done something strange, perhaps even wrong. After all, he said, his preacher had always taught that you didn't need to be baptized to be saved. Another member of their group spoke up, saying he had been baptized when he was a baby but really wasn't sure why. Knowing that Chris' church taught that a person should be baptized, they returned to him. "So, Chris, why were you baptized?"

It's important to embark on your own mission to find the truth about baptism, both for yourself and for those you one day may have the chance to bring closer to God.

This was an opportunity that did not come Chris' way very often – a chance to tell his closest friends what God has to say about baptism. The topic had never come up before, and, to say the least, he hadn't spent a lot of time practicing for this moment. But he knew this was a valuable opportunity to "give a defense" for what he believed (1 Peter 3:15) and maybe even bring his friends closer to God. His friends were listening, and Chris had a chance to speak. He gathered himself, took one more sip of his coffee as he said a quick prayer in his mind, and began trying to explain.

Have you ever found yourself in this type of situation – asked what you believe about baptism or salvation? If you haven't yet, you certainly will. It may be in the local cafe against the backdrop of a relaxing fall evening. It may be on a car trip downtown, at a get-together in your living room, or in the break room at work. Whenever they arise, these opportunities are usually unplanned and, sadly, often squandered. To make the most of them, we must know what the Bible says beforehand and know it well enough to explain it.

With that thought in mind, it's important to embark on your own mission to find the truth about baptism, both for yourself and for those you one day may have the chance to bring closer to God. One needs to know what God says about this controversial topic. But before diving headfirst into a discussion about it, it's wise first to prepare yourself by considering a valuable phrase found in Ephesians 4:15: "speaking the truth in love." What an important idea! We must first know the truth to speak it. And realizing the importance (and sensitivity) of the topic, we also must speak it in love. Let's consider these two basic principles as they relate to our study of baptism.

Importance of Truth When Discussing Baptism

Naturally, I would hope that a determination to find the truth and tell it to others would be desired by all of us, no matter what the topic was being discussed. However, I would suggest that finding and presenting the truth about the subject of baptism are more important endeavors than most. It's important not only because we must decide individually what to do about baptism in our own lives but also because what we believe about baptism will likely influence those around us.

For example, let's imagine an honest, truth-seeking friend comes to me to talk about faith. This friend has decided he needs to get his life right and asks me what he must do to be saved. What do I tell him? Should baptism be part of my response or not? How do I know? Even if I fully believed what I was saying were true, if my answer is not God's answer, what kind of effect would I be having on his spiritual – and possibly eternal – life? I might be hindering him from obeying God and receiving salvation. That's a sad thought – and certainly not a situation in which I would want to find myself.

Further, let's imagine a friend from church comes to me with questions about his baptism. He explains that he was "baptized" as a baby, which naturally meant that he had no control or say in the matter. Because he had not known why he was going into the water at the time and, therefore, did so without an understanding faith, he now wonders whether his baptism was acceptable to God. What do I tell him? Do I encourage him to be baptized with an understanding faith or tell him that as long as he had been in water with the right words spoken over him, he was fine? What are my reasons for either answer? Certainly we will not always know the right thing to say when talking to others, and often we won't have all the answers, but we surely want to do the best we can. The point is clear: The matter of baptism is tied to eternal salvation, and therefore it is one we need to understand as well as we possibly can – for ourselves and for others.

Another reason why it's important for us to discover the truth about baptism for ourselves is that the religious world at large offers so many different views about it. Whom are we going to listen to? Will we simply take someone else's word for it? You may be the smartest, kindest person in the world, but I won't blindly accept what you say if it's going to affect my eternal destiny. After all, even the smartest among us can be wrong sometimes. As we search for the correct teaching, therefore, we must filter through the various viewpoints offered by the world – and there are many of them. Many believe that baptism is necessary for salvation. Others believe baptism is only an option, a symbol of salvation already received. Some believe that baptism is full immersion in water, whereas others believe baptism can be done by sprinkling or pouring. Some believe baptism must be done with the right purpose. Still others believe that as long as a person undergoes a religious act involving water and calls it "baptism," then it doesn't matter whether the person understands what he or she is doing. Clearly, not all of these views can be right.

How can we possibly know the truth with so many competing voices? Should we just throw up our hands and give up? Of course not! We must remember that the only true standard is the Bible. We must be determined to listen to what the Bible says, realizing that it is the only 100 percent trustworthy religious guide. As we consider various viewpoints during our study, we must compare each of them to Scripture, always using the Bible as our standard of truth.

Look at the example of the Bereans in Acts 17:11. They were glad to listen to anything Paul had to say, but they wouldn't accept it for themselves unless it was confirmed by Scripture. That's the right attitude. Because the teachings of the Bible will judge us, we must let them be our guide. If we don't, we risk allowing someone else's mistake to keep us from knowing what God wants. Standing where God stands on this matter is extremely important. Why? Because what we find the Bible to say about baptism will significantly affect our own spiritual future and potentially the spiritual future of those around us.

Importance of Love When Discussing Baptism

As we've seen, people have many different ideas about baptism. What usually happens when people begin discussing topics about which they disagree? Arguments. Shouting. Hurt feelings. This is the case with almost any controversial topic, and religion is no different – especially when we start talking about issues of salvation (an extremely important subject but also an extremely sensitive one). Sadly, many harsh words have been exchanged through the years during discussions about baptism. No doubt friendships have been broken, churches have been split and enemies have been made. So what can we do to avoid such outcomes? We must show people an attitude that is not argumentative or self-serving. But *As we search for the correct teaching, we must filter through the various viewpoints offered by the world.* aren't we supposed to teach the truth boldly? Yes, we are, but we are also supposed to teach it in love (Ephesians 4:15).

Regardless of how true something is, if it's presented in a rude or arrogant way, people will not want to listen to it. Let's say you come up to me and defiantly shout that I am totally ignorant and wrong in what I believe and that if I don't do what you tell me to do, I will find myself in hell for eternity and deserving every minute of it. Do you think I would listen to you? No way. I wouldn't care what you had to say, even if you were right. You've already injured my pride, and my ears are shut. I'm feeling backed into a corner, and I'm probably about to start shouting and arguing my way out of it. It's not enough simply to know the truth about baptism and start telling people. We must tell them with a spirit of love, keeping an attitude of humility and respect alongside our spiritual boldness.

I point this out to be very clear about the purpose of this book: We want the world (starting with ourselves) to know the Bible's teachings about baptism and salvation. We want people to be saved. We don't study baptism or any other topic just to be able to win an argument or sound smarter than someone else. This is not about finding who is wrong and who is right. We should be aware of other viewpoints so we can compare them to Scripture, but our chief goal is not to start pointing fingers. Our goal is to find the truth so that we can prepare ourselves to get to heaven and help others do the same, not to insult those who have not been taught what the Bible says.

As we study our way through the Bible's teachings about baptism, we should remember to do so with a spirit of love. My hope is for this book to present the truth simply in a way that is clear and respectful. Together we will stand up for truth and discover some misconceptions often found in the religious world, but we will not be demeaning or arrogant about it. We will not laugh at the ignorance of those who have not been taught the truth on this matter. Instead, we will be respectful and fair about others' viewpoints as we try to fulfill our God-given obligation to find and stand up for the truth. The world has many sincere people who need to hear what the Bible says about baptism; let's not turn them off with poor attitudes. Let's present the truth to them boldly but with a spirit of love.

And So We Begin ...

With our overall goals and challenges now firmly in mind, we can look to the plan for the rest of this book. Section 1 of the book is an introduction to and discussion of the New Testament's teachings about baptism. After laying that foundation, we'll move to Section 2, where we'll consider common questions and objections to the importance of baptism. This study will help us get a broader perspective on the Bible's teaching about the relationship between baptism and salvation. Finally, Section 3 of our study will draw some final conclusions about how we should apply what we've learned about baptism. My prayer is that as we cross the finish line in the next 12 chapters, we will all have a greater understanding of God's will.

Clearly, we are beginning a study of utmost importance. Some difficult questions will be asked, but the truth about baptism is a message we need to know and the world needs to hear. Let us approach it with eagerness and humility. This topic is important to every single person in the world – including each one of us. At some point in our lives, we must make our own decision about baptism, and when that time comes (if it hasn't come already), we must make a choice that will decide what spiritual direction our lives will take. Will we have the knowledge to make the right decision? At other times in our lives, we will be asked about baptism. When those times come, we will have an opportunity to show someone God's will for his life. Will we be ready? I pray this study will help you in all these situations.

Discussion Questions

1. Have you ever found yourself in a discussion about baptism with your friends or family? What did you say? Did others agree or disagree?

2. Why is it important that we be able to tell people what the Bible says about baptism? What might be the result if we were to teach someone incorrectly about baptism?

3. What are some of the varying religious ideas about baptism today? Can they all be right? What is the only way to know the truth about the matter?

4. Why do you think baptism is often a sensitive topic to discuss? Do you believe God wants us to talk about the truth even if it's controversial? (Hint: Read Jude 3.)

5. Has anyone ever told you something that was true but did so with a rude or arrogant attitude? How did this affect your response to what was said?

6. Why is it so important that we be able to explain what the Bible says with an attitude of love?

7. How might a study of baptism affect the rest of your life?

Personal Reflection

1. Please take time to pray that God will bless us as we begin this study together. Pray that we will bring the right attitude to our study – one of humility and truth-seeking. Pray that we will find and understand the truth. Pray that we will be better equipped to obey and to teach others to obey the Bible's teachings about baptism and salvation. Never forget the importance of prayer in any endeavor.

2. If you have been baptized, why were you baptized? What would you say if your friends asked you that question? If someone asked you how to be saved, could you use a study of the Bible to answer him or her?

3. If you have not been baptized, why not? Have you ever thought about why others have been baptized? Have you ever studied or asked about baptism before? Be thinking about it for yourself.

BAPTISM PASSAGES:
WHAT IS BAPTISM ALL ABOUT?

Chapter 2

AND THEN THERE WAS
BAPTISM

*"John came baptizing in the wilderness and preaching a
baptism of repentance for the remission of sins" (Mark 1:4).*

I f you were to read the Bible from beginning to end, starting at Genesis
and moving straight through from one book to the next, you would
notice several things that seem to appear out of nowhere when you get to
the New Testament. Much changed from the time of the last Old Testament prophets (a period of more than 400 years, in fact). Particularly
notable is the sudden appearance of a specific means of giving one's life
to God that wasn't found in the Old Testament: baptism.

That's right. Baptism just seems to appear out of nowhere – but then
it's everywhere. John the Baptist emerged, and he was *baptizing* (Mark
1:4). Jesus as an adult appeared on the scene, and He was *baptized* by
John (vv. 9-11). Then Jesus started preaching *baptism*, and His disciples
baptized people for Him (John 3:5, 22; 4:2). After Jesus rose from the
dead, He told His disciples to go make other disciples by *baptizing*
them (Matthew 28:18-20). Peter then preached *baptism* as the means
of conversion in his great sermon on the day of Pentecost, and 3,000
people were *baptized* (Acts 2:38, 41).

Throughout the book of Acts, baptism went everywhere the gospel went. The Ethiopian eunuch, Cornelius, Lydia, the Philippian jailer and the soon-to-be great apostle Paul are a few of the well-known Bible characters who were baptized in Acts (8:38; 9:17-18; 10:48; 16:14-15, 33). Baptism became such a central part of the New Testament that Paul's letters repeatedly assumed that if you could be called a Christian, it was because you had been baptized (Romans 6:3-5; 1 Corinthians 12:13; Galatians 3:27; Ephesians 4:4-6). Around every corner in the New Testament, we find baptism waiting for us.

Search the Old Testament from top to bottom, and you won't find baptism there. Not one shred of evidence for baptism exists in the first 39 books of the Bible, but when you get to the last 27, suddenly it's in every nook and cranny. And it all starts with John. The six-month-older cousin of Jesus was a good preacher in his own right and served a special purpose in God's plan. So let's investigate the ministry of John the Baptist, attempting to find out how and why he began this whole new era in mankind's obedience to God – an era that suddenly places baptism front and center.

The "What" of John's Baptism

Exactly what does the Bible mean when it says that John was "baptizing"? What is a person doing when he baptizes someone? Whatever it is, it certainly involves water, because people were "baptized by him in the Jordan River" (Mark 1:5). Also, the baptism of Jesus resulted in His "coming up from the water" (v. 10). In fact, John himself told his listeners that he baptized them "with water" (v. 8). So baptism obviously involved water – but what did John do with the water to baptize someone? Did he simply pour water over their heads? Dunk them completely under? How about just a few sprinkles of water over the face? All of these are sometimes called "baptism" in today's religious world – but how does the Bible define "baptism"?

In a strict study of the Bible's text, we are left with the inescapable conclusion that baptism is a complete immersion in water. First, if we simply look at the meaning of the word that we translate into English as "baptism," we find definitions such as "plunge," "immerse," "dip" or "sink." (You may want to find these definitions of "baptism" in a good New Testament Greek dictionary, called a "lexicon.")

What the Bible is saying, literally, is that John taught an "immersion of repentance for the forgiveness of sins" (Mark 1:4). He literally told the crowds, "I immersed you with water" (v. 8). So every time we see the word "baptism," we could plug in words like "immerse" or "plunge" to better understand what the Bible is saying.

Second, the New Testament's descriptions of baptism call for a complete immersion under water. For example, it is called a "burial" on more than one occasion (Romans 6:3-5; Colossians 2:12). The

In a strict study of the Bible's text, we are left with the inescapable conclusion that baptism is a complete immersion in water.

act of a burial implies a complete placement of the body in the ground or tomb. Similarly, the "burial" of baptism implies a complete placement of the entire body in the water. This is why John baptized in places where "there was much water" rather than at the local well (John 3:23). This is why Jesus came "up from the water" as His baptism was completed (Mark 1:10). This is why, later in the book of Acts, Philip and the Ethiopian eunuch had to go "down into the water" for the eunuch to be baptized (Acts 8:38).

Perhaps God chose this burial in water because of the natural connection it would have with Christ's coming death, burial and resurrection (Romans 6:3-5). Or perhaps He chose it for its natural connection with washing, signifying the spiritual cleansing that takes place. Perhaps both were meant. Whatever the reasons, baptism in the Bible was a complete immersion under the water – not sprinkling, not pouring. If I'm going to stand on Scripture, I must call baptism what God calls it. And God says that John (and Jesus and His disciples) "immersed" people in water. If I'm going to be baptized, I want to do it God's way. Baptism, God's way, is immersion in water.

The "Why" of John's Baptism

Who did John think he was, starting this whole baptism idea? Did he just make it up, thinking people would enjoy getting dunked in water as a religious act? Was he trying to get attention, hoping to start the latest religious trend? Fortunately, John had much better reasons to start baptizing. First and foremost, he did it because the Creator of the universe told him to. John explained that God "sent" him "to baptize with water" (John 1:33). Luke wrote that when the Pharisees and lawyers were not baptized by John, they were "reject[ing] the counsel of God for themselves" (Luke 7:30). John didn't suddenly change the rules on his own; this was God's idea.

A second reason John baptized was to point to Jesus. In fact, John's major role in God's plan was to be the one who prepared the way for Jesus (Mark 1:2-4). God told John that whomever he saw the Spirit descend upon was the Lamb of God (John 1:31-33). Right after Jesus was baptized by John, the Spirit descended upon Jesus in the form of a dove (Luke 3:22). John

> *If I'm going to be baptized, I want to do it God's way.*

then knew that Jesus was the Lamb of God, and he began telling that truth to others (John 1:34). John's baptism also helped prepare people for Jesus because Jesus Himself would soon begin teaching baptism as the means of spiritually uniting with Him (we'll study more about that in chapter 3). So John's baptism helped point people to Jesus as the Son of God.

A third reason John baptized was to fulfill God's purpose in the lives of others. Clearly, God now wanted people to be baptized, and those who refused were rejecting God's purpose for their lives (Luke 7:30). John knew it was important to tell people what God wanted them to do. In fact, look at why Jesus said He was baptized: "to fulfill all righteousness" (Matthew 3:15). In other words, God's righteousness (or the "fulfilling of God's requirements") would not be shown perfectly in Him if He were not baptized. Even for the perfect Son of God, it would have been wrong to refuse to be baptized. John had to tell people, "God's plan for your life now includes baptism."

John had a job to do – a job that came straight from God Himself. Jesus later said that John was the first to preach the gospel of "the kingdom of God" (Luke 16:16); he had the privilege of introducing the world to God's new plan – a plan that pointed to Jesus and His kingdom and a plan that featured baptism as a means of fulfilling God's purpose in man's life. What a responsibility! It was a message that had never been heard before, even in the many great writings of the Old Testament. But it was a message that would start changing the world forever.

The End of John's Baptism

John's heyday didn't last forever. It wasn't supposed to. He knew his role was to point others to Christ and then to sit back and let Jesus increase as he decreased (John 3:30). John showed his sincere humility when he even said he "rejoiced" to see Jesus taking center stage as he saw himself quietly exiting stage right (vv. 27-29). John was killed by Herod because of John's bold stand against sin (Mark 6:14-29), and Jesus went on to become the Savior of the world. Later, the apostles made clear that John's baptism was no longer in effect and that Christ's baptism had become the means of fulfilling God's purpose (Acts 19:1-5).

John's baptism had been temporary, but it had played an important role in God's plan. In fact, many aspects of John's baptism were continued in the baptism of Christ. Both baptisms were immersions in water. Both were from God. Both demanded repentance on the part of the one being baptized (in fact, in reading Luke 3:7-14, it seems that John refused to baptize those who weren't ready to repent). Both were for the forgiveness of sins. The two baptisms were very similar. But what were the differences? That's where we're heading next as we explore the baptism of Christ in more detail. The major difference between John's baptism and Christ's baptism is that Christ's baptism truly connects man with God in a special way. And, as we will see in the next chapter, it all starts by connecting with Jesus Himself.

Discussion Questions

1. Can you name some people who were baptized and/or taught about baptism in the Bible? Does baptism seem important based on how often it appears in the Bible?

2. Besides complete immersion in water, what are some of the various acts that are called "baptism" in the religious world? Could you explain to someone how we know baptism in the Bible means full immersion in water?

3. Why do you think God chose immersion in water to play an important part in His plan? Could the death, burial and resurrection of Christ play a role? (See Romans 6:3-5 and Colossians 2:12.)

4. Why did John suddenly begin baptizing when the Bible had never mentioned anything about it before his time?

5. Why was Jesus baptized? Does the fact that Jesus was baptized say anything about its importance?

6. What are some similarities and differences between John's baptism and Christ's baptism? Which baptism is meant for our lives today? (Hint: Read Acts 19:1-5.)

Personal Reflection

1. Repentance is an important part of baptism. Read Luke 3:7-14. What did John demand of those he baptized? What changes do you think God demands of us?

2. John was the type of person who was willing to stand up for what God wanted, no matter how unpopular it was. He even stood up to Herod, king of Judea, because the king was involved in an improper marriage (Mark 6:14-29). Are you bold enough to speak God's truth to the world even when it's not popular?

3. John also was willing to sacrifice himself for God. Look at how simple his life was according to Mark 1:6. Have you sacrificed anything for God?

Chapter 3

BAPTISM IS ABOUT ...
JESUS

*"And he commanded them to be baptized in the
name of the Lord" (Acts 10:48).*

I'm sure everyone has had a teacher like Ms. Bowman. You know
the type: extremely committed, extremely intelligent and, worst of
all, extremely tough. She was my high school history teacher. Most of
my teachers would provide the class a review the day before the test – a
review that essentially told us exactly what the test questions would
be. But Ms. Bowman was different. Her "review" sounded more like,
"Just know everything I've lectured about since the last test." Wow,
thanks. So many pages of notes filled with names, battles, places and
events – where would I start?

Eventually we picked up on the not-so-difficult pattern. Ms. Bowman's tests didn't ask about every little detail. Rather, she graded
us on how well we knew the highlights, the most important events.
So we began listening not only to what Ms. Bowman lectured about
but especially to the things on which she placed more emphasis. She
would repeat certain things, refer back to them and mention them more
than once. The light would finally go on: "She keeps mentioning the

Stamp Act. I think I'd better study and remember that." And so we learned: When Ms. Bowman kept repeating something, that meant it was important.

The New Testament includes so many references to baptism that it's difficult to know where to start. What should we emphasize first? How can we know what God thinks is most important about baptism? I suggest we take a lesson from my high school history class: If God repeats something over and over, He's trying to emphasize it.

How does this realization help us in our study of baptism? Someday when you have an extra couple of hours, I've got a little exercise for you. Set aside the cell phone or the remote control, and pull out a good Bible concordance. Find all the verses in the New Testament that talk about Christ's baptism, and see how the Bible describes it. You'll find several common words that jump out at you, such as "water," "forgiveness," "Spirit" and "burial." But do you know what you'll find mentioned in baptism contexts more than anything else in the Bible? Jesus Himself. Time after time, the New Testament descriptions of baptism refer to Jesus in one way or another:

If God repeats something over and over, He's trying to emphasize it.

• Baptism "in the name of the Father and of the Son and of the Holy Spirit" (Matthew 28:19).
• Baptism "in the name of Jesus Christ" (Acts 2:38).
• Baptism "in the name of the Lord" (Acts 10:48).
• Baptism "in the name of the Lord Jesus" (Acts 8:16; 19:5).
• Baptism "into Christ Jesus" (Romans 6:3; Galatians 3:27).
• Baptism is into the death of Jesus (Romans 6:3; Colossians 2:12).
• Baptism clothes us with Christ, or "puts on Christ" (Galatians 3:27).
• Baptism puts us in the one body of Christ (1 Corinthians 12:12-13).
• In baptism we are raised up with Jesus (Colossians 2:12).
• Baptism saves us through the resurrection of Jesus Christ (1 Peter 3:21).

On and on it goes. Far more than anything else, the Bible associates baptism with Jesus – which tells me that the most important thing to know about baptism is that it has to do with Jesus. But what does that mean?

What's in a Name?

The book of 1 Corinthians helps us begin to understand what it meant to be baptized in someone's name during biblical times. As Paul wrote this letter, he barely could believe what he had heard. Apparently, the Corinthian church was arguing and dividing into cliques, with each clique claiming to be followers of a different preacher. Some claimed to be followers of the teachings of Paul, others of Apollos, Peter or simply followers of Christ. Paul wouldn't stand for it. As he began writing, he scolded the Corinthians for claiming to be followers of anyone other than Christ, asking three rhetorical questions, all assuming an obvious "no" answer: "Is Christ divided? Was Paul crucified for you? Or were you baptized in the name of Paul?" (1 Corinthians 1:13).

That last question tells us something about what it meant to be baptized in someone's name. Listen to Paul's logic: Don't claim to be a follower of Paul; you weren't baptized in the name of Paul. What's the implied meaning? If you *had* been baptized in the name of Paul, then you could call yourself a follower of Paul. Therefore, if you were baptized in someone's name in biblical times, you were committing yourself to following his teachings. You were aligning yourself with the religious teacher whose baptism you accepted. Those who were baptized in John's baptism committed themselves to following John's teaching. Those baptized in Christ's name were committing themselves to following Christ's teaching. If Paul had baptized people in his own name, he would have been asking people to follow him.

This idea also seems to be implied in 1 Corinthians 10:2, where Paul said the Israelites were "baptized into Moses." Were the Israelites ever actually baptized? No. But Paul is trying to make a connection between the Israelites and the Corinthian Christians. His point: The Israelites had passed through water – in the cloud of God's presence (Exodus 14:19-20) and the parting of the Red Sea (vv. 21-22) – to become followers of Moses, their deliverer from Egypt. In similar fashion, Paul implies, the Corinthians literally had passed through water in baptism to become followers of Christ, their deliverer from sin. Here we see that to be baptized "into" Christ is the same idea as baptism "in the name of" Christ: a baptism in which you commit to become a follower of Jesus.

This idea also may explain why John the Baptist's followers became jealous when people first began to be baptized by Jesus (John 3:26). When Jesus began baptizing people, it meant He was drawing them to be His own disciples ("disciple" means "follower"). John's disciples were upset not because Jesus was baptizing people into John's baptism but because Jesus was baptizing people into His own baptism – an offer to follow Jesus rather than John. John explained to them that Jesus was greater than he and that Jesus' work would increase far beyond his own (vv. 27-30). A short time later the Bible says Jesus had "baptized more disciples than John" (4:1). Whose disciples were they becoming? Disciples of Jesus. How did He make them His disciples? He baptized them. And after He was risen from the grave, Jesus commanded His chosen apostles to continue that same task:

> Go therefore and make disciples of all the nations, baptizing them in the name of the Father and of the Son and of the Holy Spirit, teaching them to observe all things that I have commanded you (Matthew 28:19-20).

How do people become followers of Jesus (and, therefore, followers of the Father and the Spirit as well)? The passage above gives three steps: They are taught about Jesus, baptized in the name of God and taught further to follow Christ's teachings. Accepting Jesus' baptism means spiritually uniting one's self with His teaching and leadership and – because He taught that He is God's own Son – acknowledging Him as one's Lord.

I Stand With Jesus

From all we have just read, it is clear that when the apostles in the book of Acts commanded their listeners to "be baptized in the name of Jesus Christ" (Acts 2:38; 10:48; 19:5), they were saying that baptism would unite people with Jesus. Those being baptized were committing themselves to following Jesus' message of the kingdom: loving God, loving your neighbor, living a holy life and accepting Christ as God's Son. They were spiritually uniting themselves with Jesus.

Of course, by the time the apostles spoke those words, being united with Jesus had come to mean much more than just following His teachings, as it may have meant while Jesus was living on earth. For by then, Jesus had become a sacrifice for the sins of all mankind in dying a perfect death on the cross. He had conquered death by rising from the grave. He had ascended to the right hand of God and had sent the Spirit into the world to glorify Him. Therefore, uniting with Jesus had taken on a whole new meaning. Not only were Christians uniting themselves with His *teachings*, but they also were uniting themselves with His *blessings*, accomplished through His death, burial and resurrection. The apostles were asking people

> *When we commit ourselves to becoming a follower of Jesus through baptism in His name, we unite ourselves with His teachings and His blessings.*

to change their lives and their eternities through the commitment and blessings of Christ's baptism. Thousands of souls accepted that offer, often being baptized immediately after hearing the message (Acts 2:41; 16:33; 19:5). They took their stand with Jesus and began living for Him (2:42-47); it was the most important commitment they ever made.

So there's our starting point: Throughout the New Testament, the emphasis of baptism is on Jesus. His name is associated with descriptions of baptism more than anything else. Baptism is in the name of, or into, Jesus Christ. It is about uniting with Him. It says to God and the world, "I stand with Jesus." And when we commit ourselves to become a follower of Jesus through baptism in His name, we unite ourselves with His teachings and His blessings.

And what are those blessings? That's our next step. Ephesians 1:3 says "every spiritual blessing" is "in Christ." We'll list and discuss several of them in Chapter 5. But first, in Chapter 4, we'll focus on only one: a blessing promised even in the waters of John's baptism, but a blessing that could take on full significance only through Christ's death. Although the Bible says many other blessings are given in baptism, this one is presented to unbelievers as a focal point for understanding the meaning of baptism. It's the blessing of forgiveness. After all, if anything goes hand in hand with the message of Jesus, it is forgiveness.

Discussion Questions

1. Do you agree that we should pay special attention to the ideas that the Bible repeatedly emphasizes? Does that mean we can ignore teachings that are given only once?

2. What are some ideas the Bible associates with baptism? Which one appears in Scripture more than any others? What does this tell us about the emphasis of baptism?

3. What did it mean in the Bible to be baptized in someone's name?

4. While here on earth, do you think Jesus was teaching John's baptism or His own baptism? Why? Does the jealousy of John's disciples give us a hint?

5. What are some of the teachings of Jesus that we commit to follow when we are baptized? (Some good places to start are Matthew 5–7 and 22:36-40.)

6. How did Christ's baptism take on new meaning after He had died and risen from the dead? What are some of the blessings we receive when we unite ourselves with the risen Jesus in baptism?

Personal Reflection

1. Read Luke 14:25-33. Jesus said we must not become His follower unless we can follow through on the commitment we are making to Him. Baptism is not something to take lightly. If you are thinking about being baptized, ask yourself, "Am I ready for this lifelong commitment to the teachings of Jesus?" If you have already been baptized, ask yourself, "Am I trying to live up to that great commitment I made at my baptism?"

2. Read Luke 9:57-62. What are some excuses people make that keep them from following Jesus? What excuses do you find yourself making?

Chapter 4

BAPTISM IS ABOUT ...
FORGIVENESS IN JESUS

"Then Peter said to them, 'Repent, and let every one of you be baptized in the name of Jesus Christ for the remission of sins; and you shall receive the gift of the Holy Spirit'" *(Acts 2:38).*

Jerusalem was still abuzz. The city was bursting at the seams with visitors who had come for the Pentecost feast, and everywhere people were talking about the amazing events earlier that day. It had all started that morning when a loud, violent wind had shrieked into the city, strangely focusing its force on one particular house. Crowds gathered quickly to see what had happened. From the house emerged 12 men who were claiming that God's Spirit had come upon them in the form of fiery tongues, giving them the ability to speak in other languages. And these men were not just claiming it – they were doing it!

People from all over the map heard their own languages as these men spoke, resulting in both amazement and confusion. How could this happen? These men were unmistakably from Galilee, the poorer region to the north; they could not have studied so many languages.

Could they be telling the truth? Some even began making light of the bizarre situation, suggesting the 12 men were simply drunk. The only thing clear was that something unique was happening.

Then one of the 12 men stepped forward and quieted the crowd. It was Peter, one of the apostles who had followed Jesus of Nazareth. Everyone knew about Jesus. He had claimed to be the Messiah, and for that claim He was crucified during the time of the Passover feast nearly two months earlier. The story of His death and the claims about His missing body had been the main topic of conversation among the departing Passover crowds, and that story had been fresh on everyone's minds as they had returned for Pentecost. Now at the center of this amazing event was one of Jesus' followers, speaking up to explain what was happening. I imagine you could have heard a pin drop.

Peter gave a sermon the crowd would never forget, combining the words of their beloved Old Testament prophets with what their own eyes had seen. He began with the prophet Joel, who had predicted the Spirit would be poured out on men, and claimed that the crowd was witnessing a fulfillment of Joel's prophecy.

Then Peter started talking about Jesus. He reminded the people about all the miracles Jesus had done, which no one could deny. He reminded them that they had watched – some had even cheered – as Jesus was condemned and nailed to a cross. He claimed that Jesus had risen from death, fulfilling a prophecy of David. Now, Peter said, Jesus had ascended to the right hand of God (fulfilling another prophecy of David) and had poured out the Holy Spirit, which they were all witnessing. Then came Peter's pointed conclusion: "Therefore let all the house of Israel know assuredly that God has made this Jesus, whom you crucified, both Lord and Christ" (Acts 2:36).

What followed was like nothing anyone had ever seen. The people realized their shame, maybe even gasped, as it became obvious Peter was right. The Bible says they were cut to the heart. And so they pleaded: What should we do? How can we make up for our sin against Jesus? Peter answered in Acts 2:38: "Repent, and let every one of you be baptized in the name of Jesus Christ for the remission of sins; and you shall receive the gift of the Holy Spirit."

For the Forgiveness of Sins

Peter told the crowd they needed to repent – to "turn around" and begin accepting Jesus rather than rejecting Him. As part of that repentance, Peter said they needed to be baptized in Jesus' name for the remission (forgiveness) of their sins. (He also added something about the Holy Spirit, which we will discuss in chapter 5.) What did he mean in saying that Christ's baptism is "for the forgiveness of sins"?

For the answer we go back to Jesus Himself. Jesus came to the earth for several important reasons. He came to bring the message of God's new kingdom, the church. He came to show the world an example of how to live. He came to *Jesus came to earth to become a sacrifice for the sins of mankind.* show the world what God was like. And He came to become a sacrifice for the sins of mankind. Man was simply too sinful and helpless to save himself – everyone needed Jesus.

As Jesus had sat around the Passover table with His apostles for the last time, He instituted what the Bible later calls the Lord's Supper. He asked the apostles to partake of the unleavened bread, telling them it represented His body, which was to be sacrificed on the cross the next day. He then took a cup, full of the juice that comes from grapes, and told the disciples: "Drink from it, all of you. For this is My blood of the new covenant, which is shed ["poured out," NIV, NASB] for many for the remission of sins" (Matthew 26:27-28).

Notice that Jesus said His blood would be poured out "for the remission of sins," the same phrase Peter used in Acts 2:38. What did Jesus mean? Was Jesus pouring out His blood because men were already forgiven? No; we've already seen that no one can be forgiven without Christ's sacrifice. Jesus was pouring out His blood so that mankind could be forgiven. No blood, no forgiveness.

So when Peter used the same phrase, saying that baptism was "for the remission of sins," it is clear what he meant. Was he saying they should be baptized because they were already forgiven? Of course not. They needed to be baptized to be forgiven of their sins. They could refuse the offer if they wanted to, but the choice was theirs: If they were willing to change, they could be baptized – and in that baptism, they would be forgiven.

Baptism and the Death of Jesus

This leads us to another question: Why did Peter believe baptism and forgiveness were so closely connected? Once again the answer is found in the sacrifice of Jesus on the cross. With the death of Jesus, the price for the sins of the world has been paid.

Yet the Bible still teaches that many people will not be saved. But if Jesus died for the sins of the whole world, why will the whole world not be saved? Clearly, not everyone receives the blessings given in the death of Christ. Jesus will not force His saving blood on us; we must accept it by our own choice. God has given the sacrifice, and He has offered us the way to unite our souls with the blessings of that sacrifice. So how do we accept His offer and allow our sins to be covered with the saving blood of Christ's death? Look at Romans 6:3: "Or do you not know that as many of us as were baptized into Christ Jesus were baptized into His death?"

As we saw in chapter 3, baptism unites us with Jesus Christ. And in Romans 6:3, Paul took that connection a little deeper: When we are united with Jesus, we are also united with His death. In the waters of baptism, our souls are covered with the blood of Jesus that was shed in His death on the cross. And here's where that final Passover meal with Jesus comes in again. Why did Jesus say His blood was to be shed? "For the forgiveness of sins." Baptism is how we receive the forgiveness of Christ's death.

Baptism and the Washing Away of Sins

When we understand how the death of Christ, forgiveness of sins and baptism relate to each other, other passages of Scripture suddenly make much more sense. For example, when Jesus appeared to Saul on the road to Damascus in Acts, Jesus told Saul that He had been sinning against Jesus Himself by persecuting the church, and He

Just as taking a bath physically washes away dirt from our bodies, being baptized spiritually washes away sin from our souls.

told Saul to go into the city and wait. When Ananias arrived to tell Saul what God wanted him to do, he said: "And now why are you waiting?

Arise and be baptized, and wash away your sins, calling on the name of the Lord" (Acts 22:16).

What was Ananias saying? Being immersed in water might wash some dirt off Paul, but how could it wash off his sins? Ananias wasn't confusing dirt and sin. He was referring to the spiritual washing that God gives us in baptism. It was just another way to say that God forgives our sins through Christ's death at baptism.

This idea of "washing our sins away" may be another reason God chose baptism as the act involved in becoming a Christian. We all understand that water washes – when our hands get dirty, we go to the sink and wash them off. When our bodies get dirty, we take a shower or a bath. Perhaps God chose baptism because it was the best way to help us understand what He does for our souls through Jesus Christ. Just as taking a bath physically washes away dirt from our bodies, being baptized spiritually washes away sin from our souls. It is a washing of forgiveness.

A Natural Connection

Jesus came and died to offer forgiveness to the world. We are baptized to unite our lives with Jesus. Therefore, it only makes sense that when we are united with Jesus, we are united with the great blessings of His death. And of all the blessings of Christ's death, forgiveness of our sins is emphasized more than any other. Jesus emphasized it at the last Passover meal. Peter emphasized its relationship to baptism in his sermon that morning at Pentecost. Ananias made the connection of baptism and forgiveness when telling Saul what God wanted him to do. A sinner can be forgiven if he will let Jesus wash his sins away – that's what the gospel is all about! At least 3,000 people discovered it on the day of Pentecost, and the world has been buzzing about it ever since.

Forgiveness is not the only blessing given through Christ at baptism, however. In chapter 5 we will explore some other blessings the Bible says are given in baptism. Before we get there, can you name some?

Discussion Questions

1. Why do you think Jesus established a "Lord's Supper" for the church to partake of regularly?

2. What are some reasons for Jesus' coming to earth? Name some of the ways He accomplished these goals.

3. If Jesus died for the whole world, why will the whole world not be saved? (See 2 Thessalonians 1:6-10.)

4. Can we be saved without the blood of Jesus that was shed in His death? When does the Bible say we are united with the death of Christ? (See Romans 6:3.)

5. In Matthew 26:28, when Jesus said that His blood would be poured out "for the remission of sins," did He mean that the world was already forgiven of its sins? Or did He mean that His blood would be shed to give forgiveness of sins? How does that help us understand what Peter said about baptism and forgiveness in Acts 2:38?

6. What sins had Saul committed before He became a Christian? How was he told to get rid of those sins?

7. Read Isaiah 59:1-2. What separates man from God? Does this tell us about the importance of forgiveness?

Personal Reflection

1. If our sins are washed away in baptism, what about the sins that we commit after we are baptized? Do we need to be baptized again? In 1 John 1:6-10, the apostle John writes about how Christians' sins continue to be forgiven. What does he say? Have you already been baptized? If so, have you been walking in the light? Do you need to confess sin?

2. What if Jesus had decided not to come to earth and die on the cross? What would be different?

Chapter 5

BAPTISM IS ABOUT …
ALL SPIRITUAL BLESSINGS IN JESUS

*"Blessed be the God and Father of our Lord Jesus Christ,
who has blessed us with every spiritual blessing in the
heavenly places in Christ" (Ephesians 1:3).*

C onsidering all the amazing things Jesus had done, it was only fitting
that He leave the world in spectacular fashion. He had performed
countless miracles. He had taught with unmatched wisdom. He had died
to a backdrop of supernatural darkness and earthquakes (Matthew 27:45-
54). He had even risen from the grave, proving beyond any doubt that
He was indeed God in the flesh. Now, 40 days after His resurrection,
He had gathered the apostles together one last time. After some final
words of instruction, this is how Luke records Christ's final moments
on earth: "Now when He had spoken these things, while they watched,
He was taken up, and a cloud received Him out of their sight" (Acts 1:9).

Can you imagine the amazement on the apostles' faces? Jesus had
simply ascended off the ground, into the clouds, and ultimately into
heaven itself. Even after all they had seen, Christ's final exit left the
apostles speechless (Acts 1:10-11). And given everything else Christ
had done, it wouldn't have felt right any other way.

The Bible says that after Jesus' grand exit, God seated Jesus "at His right hand in the heavenly places" (Ephesians 1:20). From that exalted position, Jesus has continued to be active in His mission to bring salvation to the world. Even more awe-inspiring, the Bible teaches that when we are united with Jesus in baptism, we are also united with His resurrection. Look at Colossians 2:12: "[B]uried with Him in baptism, in which you also were raised with Him through faith in the working of God, who raised Him from the dead."

Baptism is not only a joining with Christ's death but also a joining with His resurrection. As Paul put it, God has raised us up with Christ and seated us with Him in the heavenly places (Ephesians 2:6). In baptism, God spiritually seats us right next to Him. Let's consider some of the spiritual blessings given in baptism that result from being united with the resurrected Christ.

Jesus and the Church

In Ephesians 1:20-23, Paul taught that when Christ was seated at the right hand of God, He was made head over the church, which is also called His body. In other words, Christ's resurrection and ascension began His reign as King for those who are saved by spiritually uniting with Him (Colossians 1:13-14). The worldwide invitation to enter Christ's kingdom began soon after

Jesus said that no one can be part of God's saved kingdom unless he or she is "born of water and the Spirit."

Christ's ascension, on the day of Pentecost in Acts 2. Since that time, mankind has been offered an opportunity to be part of Christ's body, trusting Him to save them and to lead them.

How then do we become part of this kingdom? Jesus told Nicodemus quite explicitly what must be done: "Jesus answered, 'Most assuredly, I say to you, unless one is born of water and the Spirit, he cannot enter the kingdom of God'" (John 3:5).

Jesus said that no one can be part of God's saved kingdom unless he or she is "born of water and the Spirit." What was He talking about? In the context of the first chapters of John, "born of water" can be talking only about baptism. In John 1–4, both John and Jesus are continually teaching people to be baptized in water (John 1:25-28, 31-33; 3:22-26;

4:1-2). Even further, considering all of Christ's teachings, what else but baptism could "water" possibly refer to? Jesus was telling Nicodemus that baptism is a new birth, in which we enter God's kingdom.

Later, Paul would add that baptism makes us part of Christ's special people: "For by one Spirit we were all baptized into one body – whether Jews or Greeks, whether slaves or free – and have all been made to drink into one Spirit" (1 Corinthians 12:13).

Baptism puts us into the one body of Christ: His kingdom, His church, His chosen people. No matter what our background, language, race or class, baptism unites us as a special people of God, separate from the world.

What an amazing blessing! In baptism we become part of God's chosen people. The risen Christ becomes our leader, guiding us through this world in a special way until He finally hands us over safely to the Father at the end of time (1 Corinthians 15:24). At that point the kingdom of God will take on a whole new meaning – in heaven, the eternal home of the saved. Until that time comes, however, God's kingdom in this world is His church. When we are baptized, we become part of that kingdom, which was established through the power and guidance of the risen Jesus.

Jesus and the Spirit

During Peter's sermon on the day of Pentecost, he made an interesting connection between Christ's ascension to heaven and the miraculous Holy Spirit that was allowing the apostles to speak in tongues. He said, "Therefore being exalted to the right hand of God, and having received from the Father the promise of the Holy Spirit, He poured out this which you now see and hear" (Acts 2:33).

The risen Jesus was the one who had sent the Holy Spirit to the apostles. In fact, Jesus had promised the apostles that this would happen. The very night He was to be betrayed, He told them that He would go to the Father so that He could send the Spirit to be with the world forever (John 14:16; 16:7). For the apostles, the Spirit gave them the ability to perform miracles. They also could lay hands on people, giving others the ability to perform miracles of the Spirit (Acts 8:14-19). All of this was made possible because the risen Jesus had sent the Spirit into the world.

When the apostles died, the miraculous gifts of the Spirit disappeared also. But does that mean the Holy Spirit has nothing to do with our lives today? Certainly not. Paul wrote in 1 Corinthians 6:19 that Christians are temples of the Holy Spirit who is in them. So if the Holy Spirit is in Christians today but does not help them perform miracles, what does the Bible say He does? The Spirit sets Christians apart as belonging to Christ (Romans 8:9). He helps them get sin out of their lives (v. 13). He helps them ask God for what they truly need in life (v. 26). His presence is a down payment, promising an eternal life with God when this life is over (2 Corinthians 1:22; 5:5). The Spirit is obviously still very active, working through the inspired words of the Bible and – as 1 Corinthians 6:19 shows – in some way dwelling within the Christian.

The New Testament repeatedly connects baptism with the presence of the Holy Spirit.

So when does God send His Spirit to dwell in our hearts? Here are some verses we've already looked at, but notice now the promise of the Holy Spirit in each of them:

• In Acts 2:38, Peter promised that if the people would repent and be baptized, they would "receive the gift of the Holy Spirit."

• In John 3:5, Jesus said we must be "born of water and the Spirit."

• In 1 Corinthians 12:13, Paul said that we are all baptized "by one Spirit" and therefore "made to drink into one Spirit."

• In Matthew 28:18-20, Jesus said to baptize in the name of the Father, Son and the Holy Spirit, meaning we are united with all three in our baptism.

Clearly, the New Testament repeatedly connects baptism with the presence of the Holy Spirit. Although this does not mean we will perform miracles of the Spirit, it does mean that we become temples of the Spirit. God lives in us. He helps us as we try to live for Him. All of this is possible because in baptism we are united with the risen Jesus, God's own Son who sent the Spirit into the world.

Jesus and Eternal Life

Jesus suffered more than we could ever imagine in dying on the cross. It seemed like sin and death had won. However, His resurrection conquered both, beginning His never-ending life at the right hand of the Father. His death appeared to be a final defeat, but His resurrection instead brought about an eternal victory.

Years later, Peter wrote a letter encouraging Christians to stand firm in the face of physical persecution. He reminded them about Noah, who was surrounded by a disobedient world but was brought safely by God through the waters of the flood. With that picture of Noah and his deliverance as a type of baptism, Peter then wrote one of the Bible's clearest statements about baptism:

> There is also an antitype which now saves us – baptism (not the removal of the filth of the flesh, but the answer of a good conscience toward God), through the resurrection of Jesus Christ, who has gone into heaven and is at the right hand of God, angels and authorities and powers having been made subject to Him (1 Peter 3:21-22).

The New American Standard Bible words this passage even more clearly: "Corresponding to that, baptism now saves you – not the removal of dirt from the flesh, but an appeal to God for a good conscience – through the resurrection of Jesus Christ, who is at the right hand of God, having gone into heaven,

Christians are joined with the power of Christ's conquering resurrection when they are baptized into Him.

after angels and authorities and powers had been subjected to Him."

Peter reminded Christians that even if they suffered or lost their lives, their baptism saved them. Many Christians would be persecuted and made to suffer and die, so how were they saved? Peter was saying that their baptism saved them from sin and its punishment; they would be raised to an eternal life. How was this possible? Through the resurrection of Jesus Christ. Christians are joined with the power of Christ's conquering resurrection when they are baptized into Him. Because of His resurrection, we are saved at baptism, receiving His gift of eternal life.

So Many Blessings in Jesus

Ephesians 1:3 says that God has given us "every spiritual blessing" in Christ. We may never fully comprehend every one of those amazing blessings given to us through Jesus. After all, it is no small matter to be spiritually united with God's own Son! Although forgiveness is often emphasized in Scripture as a key blessing given through Christ's death, forgiveness is certainly not Christ's only blessing. Through His resurrection, Jesus became a King, sent the Holy Spirit and conquered death. By being baptized into Him, we unite ourselves with the blessings of His resurrection – becoming part of His kingdom, becoming a temple of the Spirit and receiving eternal life. What does all this tell us? Because of His death and resurrection, being baptized into Christ makes us the most blessed people in the world.

Discussion Questions

1. What has Jesus done since He ascended to heaven? Has He stopped being involved in trying to save the world from sin?

2. In John 3:3-5, what does Jesus say we must do to be a part of His kingdom? How do you know this passage is talking about baptism?

3. What is so special about being part of God's chosen people? What are some ways in which Jesus might be guiding or leading His church today?

4. When Jesus poured out the Spirit on the apostles, what was the result? Does the Spirit still live in Christians today, even if He does not give them power to perform miracles? If so, what does He do? When do we become temples of the Spirit?

5. What did Peter mean when he said, "Baptism now saves you"? If God wanted to tell us that baptism is for salvation, could He say it more clearly than that?

6. Name some blessings given to us through Christ. Do you think we will ever comprehend all of them?

Personal Reflection

1. Read Romans 14:10-12, which says that everyone will bow down before God at the judgment. When that moment comes and everyone

realizes the power of the resurrected Jesus, how will it feel to those who have not become part of His kingdom in life? What about those who obeyed Him in this life? What about you?

2. Read 1 Corinthians 6:19-20. If I am the temple of the Holy Spirit, how should that affect how I use my body?

3. What do you think eternity with Jesus will be like?

Chapter 6

BAPTISM IS ABOUT ...
CHANGE IN JESUS

"Therefore, if anyone is in Christ, he is a new creation;
old things have passed away; behold, all things
have become new" (2 Corinthians 5:17).

M att and Cindy were married today. They were not married yesterday or the day before or even when they woke up this morning.
But today that changed.

Matt had dated Cindy for a couple of years. They had spent a lot of
time together, becoming almost inseparable. They went out on dates
nearly every Friday night. They were dating, but they were not married. As Matt approached his college graduation, he decided that he
wanted to spend the rest of his life with Cindy. He bought a ring. One
night, during a riverside walk after a nice dinner, Matt got down on
one knee and asked Cindy to marry him. Amid the tears and smiles,
Cindy happily said yes. Matt and Cindy were engaged, but they were
still not married. More steps remained.

They spent the next year planning a wedding. Invitations, dresses,
tuxes and decorations became the subject of countless conversations.
Eventually, the wedding plans were complete and the reservations

were made. Matt and Cindy had a wedding planned, but they did not yet have a marriage.

Finally, Matt and Cindy stood before a preacher and an assembly of witnesses. They gave their vows. They exchanged rings. And finally, the preacher announced them "husband and wife." They kissed, their friends and family applauded, and they smiled like never before as they walked down the aisle hand in hand. Matt and Cindy were now married.

What had changed? Five minutes earlier they had been committed to each other, but they were not married. The change from "single" to "married" involved both a commitment and a ceremony. Now, after the ceremony, their families consider them married. The government considers them married.

The ceremony of marriage causes a big change. Paul described a change even more monumental than marriage.

God considers them married. A simple ceremony, but a big change.

Helen experienced a similar change today. She moved to the United States several years ago, going to school and eventually working in the medical field. She lived and worked with Americans, but she was not an American. She applied for citizenship and passed a test on basic American history. A date was set for her naturalization ceremony. She would soon be an American, but not yet. One more step remained.

Finally, today she stood with a large group of other immigrants, repeated a pledge of commitment to the United States, listened to several speeches about American responsibility, and was officially declared an American citizen. She smiled, and the crowd cheered because things were different now. When she awoke this morning, she was still an immigrant working in a foreign nation. But now this land is her land. She has inherited all the rights and privileges of an American citizen. A simple ceremony, but a big change.

Change, Christ and Baptism

In 2 Corinthians 5:17, Paul described a change even more monumental than marriage or citizenship. The change he had in mind was one of eternal significance: the change in one's life that comes through Jesus Christ. He said, "Therefore, if anyone is in Christ, he is a new creation."

A new creation! What in the world was Paul talking about? Christians are still people, not new creatures. There is no caterpillar-to-butterfly transformation when we go from "out of Christ" to "in Christ." Or is there? Clearly, Paul was describing a spiritual newness rather than a physical one. He was saying that there is a Grand Canyon-sized gap between the spiritual lives of those who are in Christ and those who are not. The change is so great that Paul could only describe Christians as entirely new creatures. They are spiritually different from the rest of the world.

But how does that change take place? Actually, here we can take a lesson from the wedding and citizenship analogies. After all, the Bible uses those very images when describing the Christian change. Read Ephesians 5:25-33. Paul said the relationship between Christ and the church is like a marriage. If we are members of Christ's church, we have been spiritually "married" to Christ (2 Corinthians 11:2).

Look further at Ephesians 2:19, where Paul reminded his readers about the change experienced by those who are now in Christ Jesus: "Now, therefore, you are no longer strangers and foreigners, but fellow citizens with the saints and members of the household of God."

Being "in Christ" means we have entered into a spiritual marriage contract. We have become citizens

Baptism is that special ceremony that changes us from being in the world to being in Christ.

in His kingdom. And, as we might expect, the change process is very similar. We must first decide we want to be in Christ, a decision that comes from faith in who He is. We then must take the proper steps toward making that decision a reality, which starts with a commitment to living for Him. Finally, we must go through the ceremony at which the change actually occurs.

Baptism, of course, is that special ceremony that changes us from being in the world to being in Christ. Read again Romans 6:3, where Paul wrote that we are "baptized into Christ Jesus," and Galatians 3:27, where Paul wrote that all who were "baptized into Christ have put on Christ." If you were to read the New Testament from Matthew to Revelation, only one act is described as putting us into Christ: baptism. Before baptism we are not in a spiritual relationship with Him; we are outside of His kingdom. At baptism we are put "into Christ," joining

Him in a spiritual relationship and becoming a citizen in His kingdom. And that's a big change – a "new creation" change. But what exactly changes when we are in Christ?

A Change of Status

In marriage, a person's status changes from "single" to "married." In naturalization, a person's status changes from "foreign" to "American." And in baptism into Christ,

When we are "without Christ," we have no hope. Our lives are empty. We are on our own.

a person's status changes from "unsaved" to "saved," that is, to "Christian." We take the name of Jesus Christ – after all, it is in His name we are baptized (Acts 2:38). But this change of status is more than just a name designation. It is a change of our spiritual status before God.

Again we go to Ephesians 2, where verse 12 describes our status before we were in Christ: "[A]t that time you were without Christ, being aliens from the commonwealth of Israel and strangers from the covenants of promise, having no hope and without God in the world."

Paul painted a bleak picture. When we are "without Christ," look at our status. We are excluded from God's chosen people. We have no part in the promises God gives to His children. We have no hope. We do not have God. It's a sad story to be sure. Our lives are empty. There is no hope for eternity. We are on our own.

But then we are baptized into Christ. What does the Bible say is "in Christ"? Read these verses:
• Eternal life is in Christ (1 John 5:11).
• Grace is in Christ (2 Timothy 2:1).
• Salvation and eternal glory are in Christ (2 Timothy 2:10).
• Redemption and forgiveness of sins are in Christ (Colossians 1:14).
• All spiritual blessings are in Christ (Ephesians 1:3).
To put it simply, we become saved children of God in Christ. In baptism, our status changes from excluded to chosen, from lost to saved. A simple ceremony, but a big change.

A Change of Outlook

During a marriage ceremony, we make vows of commitment: For richer or poorer, in sickness or health, we pledge to love and be faithful to our spouse. Life goes from being about me to being about us. In a U.S. naturalization ceremony, an oath of allegiance is repeated. Immigrants pledge to renounce their allegiance to foreign nations and to support and defend the Constitution against all enemies. Thereafter, the new citizen has a different outlook. The United States becomes his or her highest political allegiance. When we are baptized into Christ, we are making a similar pledge. In taking His name, we are committing ourselves to live for Christ and work for His goals in this world. Thereafter, we have a new outlook on life.

We get a hint of this new outlook in 2 Corinthians 5, the very chapter where Paul wrote that we are new creatures in Christ. For example, look at what He wrote about Christ's death in verse 15: "[A]nd He died for all, that those who live should live no longer for themselves, but for Him who died for them and rose again."

Jesus died for us – not only for forgiveness of sins but also to help us gain a new focus in life. Namely, He wants us to stop living for ourselves and start living for Him. Most people are self-centered. They will push anyone and anything out of their way to get what they want. Jesus wants us to be different. He wants us to love God above all things (Matthew 22:37-38). He wants us to love our neighbors as ourselves (v. 39). Our outlook changes from selfish and worldly to faithful and loving. When we are baptized, we pledge ourselves to a new outlook on life. A simple ceremony, but a big change.

The God of New Creations

We serve a God who makes things new. He created our amazing world out of nothing. He continues to create new physical things in His world through childbirth and the annual coming of spring. He has promised that He will one day create a new heaven and a new earth for His people. He also makes

In that new birth, we go from lost, selfish, sin-filled people to saved, caring and forgiven Christians.

new creations out of people like you and me through baptism. We are "born of water and the Spirit" (John 3:5). And in that new birth, God transforms our lives into something wonderful. We go from lost, selfish, sin-filled people to saved, caring and forgiven Christians. An empty, hollow life becomes purpose-filled and even eternal. Paul knew a big change when he saw it. New creatures indeed.

Discussion Questions

1. What are the steps to getting married? What are the steps to becoming an American citizen? How are these steps similar to those involved in becoming a Christian? Are there any Bible verses that suggest these comparisons are good ones?

2. How does the Bible say we get "into Christ"? If we are baptized "into" Christ, what are we before we are baptized?

3. How are we "new creatures" in Christ? How are Christians different from the rest of the world?

4. How would you describe the spiritual status of those who are outside of Christ? What are some spiritual blessings that come from being "in Christ"? Read Ephesians 2:11-19 for some possible answers.

5. How is baptism similar to a pledge or oath?

6. How is the world outlook of a Christian different from the outlook of an unbeliever? What are some ways in which a Christian should treat people differently than the world treats them?

7. Pretend you have a friend who is thinking about baptism. What do you tell him (or her) that baptism is all about? Why should he or she be baptized? (Consider what you've studied in Chapters 3-6.)

8. If you, yourself, haven't been baptized, consider what you've studied in Chapters 3–6. Why should you be baptized?

Personal Reflection

1. Some people don't become Christians because they believe their past is too sinful to be forgiven. Read 1 Timothy 1:15. What did Paul call himself? Did God show His power in making Paul a "new creation" in Christ? How? What does this tell you about what God can do in your life?

2. In what ways do you still "live for yourself" rather than for Christ? What can you do to give yourself more fully to Him this week?

3. What are some things God has created, is creating or will create that amaze you? Doesn't this show you that He has the power to make us new creatures for Him?

BAPTISM QUESTIONS:
WHY DOESN'T
EVERYONE BELIEVE
BAPTISM IS IMPORTANT?

Chapter 7

WHAT ABOUT
OTHER SALVATION
PASSAGES?

"The entirety of Your word is truth, And every one of Your righteous judgments endures forever" (Psalm 119:160).

In Section 1 of this book, we focused on passages that teach about baptism. Common sense tells us this was a good starting point. When you study any biblical topic, you first should read all that the Bible says about it. For example, if you were studying prayer, you would want to start by reading all the passages of Scripture that talk about prayer. If you wanted to know more about the Holy Spirit, you would start by reading every verse that mentions the Holy Spirit. Every study should begin by examining and understanding the individual passages about your particular topic.

However, any study about a biblical issue also must include a second step: a study of the broader context of Scripture. For example, a study of the Bible's teaching about prayer would lead to the broader topic of worship because prayer is a form of worship. We therefore would want to expand our study, including passages that tell us everything God has to say about worship, which will help us gain a fuller understanding of prayer. In a study of the Holy Spirit, you would quickly find yourself in broader studies about God and His Word. Passages that discuss the work of the Father and the Son would need to be considered. Passages that discuss the role of God's Word would need to be compared and contrasted with the Holy Spirit passages. Studying the broader issues alongside the specific ones helps enrich and clarify our understanding of the topic.

Therefore, we now will take that second step in our study of baptism. We have seen the baptism passages. We have seen that joining with Christ is at the center of baptism. We have seen all the blessings that accompany baptism, from forgiveness and a place in God's kingdom to a new status and an eternal life. So, with these passages plainly

Many people have their own ideas about how to receive salvation, and often these ideas are based on verses that do not mention baptism.

before us, why doesn't everyone in the religious world believe in the importance of baptism? Because baptism leads us into the broader issue of salvation. That's where this second step becomes crucial. Many people have their own ideas about how to receive salvation, and often these ideas are based on verses that do not mention baptism. For us to clarify what we have found in the baptism verses, we must now study how they relate to other biblical passages about salvation.

Other Salvation Passages

We have seen that the Bible presents baptism as a way to receive salvation. Baptism is "into Christ" (Romans 6:3; Galatians 3:27), and salvation is "in Christ Jesus" (2 Timothy 2:10). In John 3:5, Jesus said that no one can enter the kingdom of God unless he is baptized. Perhaps the clearest statement of all came from 1 Peter 3:21, where Peter wrote, "Baptism now saves you" (NASB). However, baptism is not the only act that the Bible says is necessary for salvation.

• **Faith.** First, the Bible teaches that faith is necessary for salvation. Two verses in John need to be considered. John 8:24 says, "Therefore I said to you that you will die in your sins; for if you do not believe that I am He, you will die in your sins." Here Jesus said it as plainly as it can be said: Unless we believe that Jesus is the Messiah, the Savior and Son of God, we will die in our sins. Without faith we cannot be saved.

John 3:16 says, "For God so loved the world that He gave His only begotten Son, that whoever believes in Him should not perish but have everlasting life." Here, in one of the best-known verses in the entire Bible, we are told that whoever believes in Jesus will have eternal life. So the Bible is clear: Faith brings salvation, and a lack of faith means eternal death. Can I be saved simply by faith, then, ignoring the Bible's baptism verses?

• **Repentance.** There is still more to consider. The Bible also says that repentance is necessary for salvation: "I tell you, no; but unless you repent you will all likewise perish" (Luke 13:3, 5). Jesus said that unless we repent – meaning change our lives for Him – we will perish.

Look also at what the Christians said when they heard about the conversion of Cornelius: "When they heard this, they quieted down and glorified God, saying, 'Well then, God has granted to the Gentiles also the repentance that leads to life'" (Acts 11:18 NASB). Repentance leads to life – spiritual, eternal life.

The Bible is clear: Repentance saves us, and we will perish if we refuse to repent. Can I simply repent and be saved, then, ignoring the Bible's baptism verses?

• **Confession.** Finally, the Bible also stakes our salvation on confession of our faith in Jesus. Look at these two verses:

> Therefore whoever confesses Me before men, him I will also confess before My Father who is in heaven. But whoever denies Me before men, him I will also deny before My Father who is in heaven (Jesus, in Matthew 10:32-33).

> [F]or with the heart a person believes, resulting in righteousness, and with the mouth he confesses, resulting in salvation (Paul, in Romans 10:10 NASB).

If we do not confess our faith in Christ, He will deny us. If we will confess Him, the Bible says it results in salvation. So can I simply confess Jesus and be saved, ignoring the Bible's baptism verses?

How Do They Fit Together?

Clearly, baptism is not the only human response that the Bible says brings salvation. Faith, repentance and confession are also mentioned. Does this mean that baptism is not as important as we thought? Are there actually four different ways to be saved? If so, then I can choose which response I want. I can either have faith, change my life, confess Jesus or be baptized. As long as I have done one of them, I can point to a verse that says I have salvation. Is that the way God wants us to understand these passages?

We have two choices on this issue. We can either (1) pick which verses to follow or (2) assume that they are all true and that all four responses must be demonstrated for salvation.

I believe the obvious choice is the second. All these teachings are from God. We cannot pick and choose some verses to follow while ignoring others. All four responses are said to lead to salvation, but that does not mean that there are four different paths to salvation. Don't forget: The above verses also stated that if we lack any of the four, we are lost. If I do not believe Jesus is the Son of God, John 8:24 says I am lost. If I have not repented of my sins, Luke 13:3 says I am lost. If I have not confessed my faith in Jesus, Matthew 10:32-33 says I am lost. If I have not been baptized, John 3:5 says I am lost. All four must be done. And so, when all four are joined together in my life, God grants me the gift of salvation, just as He has promised.

We cannot pick and choose some verses to follow while ignoring others.

When Do They Fit Together?

Let's not look at these four responses to Christianity as if they are four separate "steps" taken at different times that will eventually fulfill God's checklist for salvation. In the Bible all four go together quite naturally in the act of baptism. You see, biblical baptism involves the presence of the other three responses. Read Colossians 2:12: "[B]uried with Him in baptism, in which you also were raised with Him through faith in the working of God, who raised Him from the dead."

How are we raised up with Christ in baptism? Through faith. Unless I am baptized with a sincere faith in God, then I am simply getting wet. Faith and baptism are not different paths to salvation – they go hand in hand.

The same can be said of repentance. Remember what Romans 6:4 said was the result of our baptism: "Therefore we were buried with Him through baptism into death, that just as Christ was raised from the dead by the glory of the Father, even so we also should walk in newness of life."

Baptism is a commitment to walk in newness of life, or repentance. Repentance and baptism are not different paths to salvation – they go together.

As you might guess, confession of one's faith accompanies baptism as well. Not only is the very act of baptism a public showing of one's faith, but baptism in the Bible was also often accompanied by a verbal confession of faith in Jesus as God's Son. Most translations of the Bible include Acts 8:37, in which the Ethiopian nobleman says, "I believe that Jesus Christ is the Son of God." In verse 38, then, Philip takes him down in the water and baptizes him. Later in the Bible, Paul was probably talking about a baptism confession when he reminded Timothy that he had "confessed the good confession in the presence of many witnesses" (1 Timothy 6:12). What was that confession? That Jesus Christ is King, the Son of God (Luke 23:1-3; 1 Timothy 6:13). Baptism involves a public confession of one's faith that Jesus is God's Son. Confession and baptism are not different paths to salvation – they go together.

More Than Just Water

As we begin to pull together all the Bible's teachings about salvation, we find that it is important to follow each and every verse. Sadly, many people miss this simple logic. One cannot decide to follow the faith passages and ignore the repentance passages. One cannot follow the confession passages and ignore the baptism passages. Each requirement stands on its own, and all are necessary to receiving God's gift of salvation.

As we begin to pull together all the Bible's teachings about salvation, we find that it is important to follow each and every verse.

Therefore, we also must remember that immersion in water does not save us by itself. Baptism must be done with a heart of faith, a commitment to repent of sins and a public acknowledgement of faith. Notice, however, that baptism is the actual point at which we are saved, because baptism is the culminating event in which all of God's requirements are met. The conversion event of baptism includes faith, repentance and confession, all united in perfect harmony. By simply deciding to listen to all that God has told us about salvation, we have already enriched our understanding of baptism. However, more questions are yet to be answered.

Discussion Questions

1. Whenever you study any biblical topic, what is the first thing you should do? Should you stop after completing this first step? Why or why not?

2. Why do some people believe baptism is not essential for salvation when the baptism verses are so clear? What other verses might they be focusing on?

3. Why is it important to follow everything God says about salvation? Why can we not ignore some verses?

4. What responses are necessary for us to receive salvation? Must we do all of them before God gives us salvation? What verses support your answers?

5. How does biblical baptism also include faith, repentance and confession?

6. What is the "good confession" made at baptism? (Read 1 Timothy 6:12-13; Luke 23:1-3 and Acts 8:36-38.)

7. Are we saved when we are baptized? Why or why not?

Personal Reflection

1. We have read verses that emphasize the importance of faith, repentance, confession and baptism. Why not take the time to memorize

them? One day someone may ask you what the Bible says must be done to be saved. Wouldn't it be great to be able to tell them confidently?

2. Another type of confession also is found in the Bible: confession of one's sins. This is done by Christians who have sinned and need forgiveness. Read James 5:16 and 1 John 1:9. Do you need to confess your sins?

Chapter 8

WHAT ABOUT
SALVATION BY
FAITH ONLY?

"What does it profit, my brethren, if someone says he has faith but does not have works? Can faith save him?" (James 2:14).

I was flipping through TV stations, and a preacher caught my eye. He was speaking before a very large crowd – in the thousands – and it wasn't hard to see why. He was an outstanding speaker. He had great things to say about God and the Bible and how we should live our lives. I agreed with one thing he said, and then another, and I began to think, "This guy is doing a great job teaching the Bible!" Before I knew it, I had listened to the last 15 minutes of his sermon. And there, at the end of the sermon, is where things got a little hazy.

Within churches of Christ, we typically end the sermon with a public offer of Christ's invitation. The preacher briefly explains what the Bible says we must do to be saved, and then he encourages sinners to obey the gospel and receive salvation. So as I watched the preacher on television, I expected that I knew what he would say. He would talk about faith, repentance, confession and the conversion event of baptism, much the way we studied it in our last chapter.

But something strange happened as this Bible-believing preacher offered his version of the invitation. He told his listeners they needed to believe in Jesus to be saved, and he quoted John 3:16. I nodded in agreement and tried to guess what passages he might use to emphasize confession or repentance next. But then he jumped the tracks. He said something about saying a prayer to Jesus, asking that He come into your heart. I began to wonder what verses taught this idea, but no Scripture was given for it. He went on to say that after one's prayer to Jesus, you could be sure you were saved because the Bible says we are saved by faith alone. And then he stopped. No repentance, no confession of faith, no baptism into Christ for forgiveness of sins.

I was confused. How could he end the sermon like that? Didn't Peter end his sermons by telling his listeners to be baptized (Acts 2:38; 10:48)? Didn't Paul's sermons end with people being baptized (Acts 16:13-15, 32-33; 18:8)? I didn't understand how a sermon could end by telling people that faith was all they needed, or at most a prayer. I sat there, gazing at the television. I felt disappointed by the preacher who I thought had done such a great job of teaching the Bible, but when it came to salvation, he seemed to leave a lot of the Bible out of it.

As we have continued our study of baptism, we've been brought slowly into the deeper waters of studying salvation. And out here we find a lot of people drifting around who don't believe what we've studied about baptism and salvation. In fact, the teachings of that TV preacher are probably the most common ones you'll hear: All you need to be saved by Jesus is faith. Faith alone saves and nothing else. These individuals will quote verses like John 3:16, and then they will stop. They are good, sincere people, but they are convinced that when the Bible says we are saved by faith, they need to go no further. (Chapter 7 showed that such thinking is not the best way to study salvation.)

Repentance, confession and baptism might be nice, but in many people's minds, they have nothing to do with salvation. Considering all the passages we have read about God's saving us in the act of baptism, I suspect something must be wrong with the teaching of faith-only salvation. Let's take a few minutes and see what the Bible says about it.

The Bible and "Faith Only"

Many passages in the Bible emphasize the importance of faith, but only one passage mentions the idea of faith only: James 2:14-26. In verse 14, James began by asking the very question we are asking: "What does it profit, my brethren, if someone says he has faith but does not have works? Can faith save him?"

This is the key question James was asking: Can faith by itself save someone? He answered in James 2:17: "Thus also faith by itself, if it does not have works, is dead."

James dealt a quick deathblow to the idea that faith saves us by itself. Faith by itself is dead, he said. James went on to give the example of Abraham, who the Bible says was declared righteous (saved) because of his faith (Genesis 15:6). But as James pointed out, Abraham's faith saved him because it was united with obedience to God's commands. God told Abraham to sacrifice Isaac, and when Abraham acted on that command, he demonstrated evidence that he not only had faith but also had obedient faith. James described it this way in 2:22: "Do you see that faith was working together with his works, and by works faith was made perfect?"

James dealt a quick deathblow to the idea that faith saves us by itself.

Clearly, the only saving faith is obedient faith. And in James 2:24, we find the only verse in the Bible that mentions faith only: "You see then that a man is justified by works, and not by faith only."

Read it again. Does it sound like faith saves us by itself? James said we are justified ("justified" means "declared innocent") by our works and not by faith alone.

They Had Faith, But Were They Saved?

If James' teaching that "faith without works is dead" is not enough to convince us (James 2:17, 26), the Bible gives several examples of people who had faith but were not saved. If faith saves us by itself, there would be no such thing as an unsaved believer.

In John 12, Jesus had been preaching to the crowds in Jerusalem, encouraging them to believe in Him as the Light of the world

(vv. 35-36). Verse 37 says many people did not believe although they had seen the signs. But then we read in John 12:42-43:

> Nevertheless even among the rulers many believed in Him, but because of the Pharisees they did not confess Him, lest they should be put out of the synagogue; for they loved the praise of men more than the praise of God.

This passage specifically says that many of the rulers believed in Jesus, which meant they had faith. But does it sound like they were saved? It says they refused to confess Him – and let's not forget what Jesus said in Matthew 10:32-33 about those who refuse to confess Him:

> Therefore whoever confesses Me before men, him I will also confess before My Father who is in heaven. But whoever denies Me before men, him I will also deny before My Father who is in heaven.

Are you saved if you refuse to confess Christ? Jesus says no. Although the rulers of John 12 believed, they refused to confess Jesus and therefore were not saved. Their faith was not an obedient faith. Faith alone was not enough to save them.

In John 8, Jesus again was preaching to the crowds in Jerusalem. Verse 31 tells us that He began a discussion with the Jews "who believed Him." As the conversation goes on, however, we see that these believers obviously were not obeying Christ's teachings on how to live. Read what Jesus said to

The Bible gives several examples of people who had faith but were not saved. If faith saves us by itself, there would be no such thing as an unsaved believer.

them in John 8:44: "You are of your father the devil, and the desires of your father you want to do."

How could Jesus call these believers children of the devil? He said it was because they wanted to do the work of the devil. Their belief was a "faith only" belief and was not combined with obedience. Jesus therefore said that they were of the devil. Does that sound like they were saved? Certainly not. Faith alone was not enough to save them.

Another example was given in James 2. After James stated that faith without works is dead, he mentioned a group that everyone would admit is lost: the demons. In verse 19 he said, "You believe that there is one God. You do well. Even the demons believe – and tremble!"

Even the demons believe in God. So does Satan. Does that mean the demons and Satan are saved? Of course not – and that was James' point: Faith by itself is not enough to save.

Salvation by Faith

Clearly, faith-only salvation is not a biblical teaching. But one thing must be made clear. The Bible does say that we are saved by faith, as we see in passages like Ephesians 2:8 and Romans 3:22. How does that make sense? How can Scripture say we are saved by faith, and yet we have seen examples in the New Testament of people who had faith but were not saved? Obviously, the Bible makes a distinction between dead faith and obedient faith. James 2 says that faith without action (faith only) is dead faith. But when faith obeys God, it becomes living faith.

Take some time to read through Hebrews 11, which is sometimes called the "hall of faith." There the Bible illustrates what saving faith looks like. In every example, men and women of faith are people who put their faith into action. Are we saved by faith only? Not at all. But are we saved by faith? Yes. Living, active, obedient faith.

And to return to the main topic of our study, what is the first step at which our faith becomes obedient faith? When we become a follower of Jesus. And what does the New Testament say is the way to acknowledge we are followers of Jesus? Baptism. Faith alone gets us nowhere, but when our faith in Christ leads us to become a Christian God's way – by being baptized into Christ – it becomes living, active, obedient, saving faith.

Discussion Questions

1. Have you ever heard a preacher teach that faith is all that's needed to be saved or that all a person needs to do is say a prayer? What did you think about it? Can preachers (even great ones) be wrong sometimes?

2. Read Acts 2:38 and 10:48. When Peter completed his sermons, what did he tell people they needed to do? How is that different from what we often hear from many preachers in the religious world today?

3. What does James 2 say about the idea of faith only? How does the example of Abraham demonstrate what living faith is?

4. Can you give some examples in the Bible of people who believed but were not saved?

5. The Bible does not say that we are saved by faith only, but does it say that we are saved by faith? If faith alone is dead faith, what type of faith saves us?

6. Read through Hebrews 11. What do these examples of faithful people tell us about saving faith? What is your favorite example in this chapter?

7. Read Acts 2:40-41; 8:12, 35-36; 16:14-15, 32-33. What do these examples tell us was the first step of faith in the New Testament? Should that be our first step of faith today?

Personal Reflection

1. Imagine that God were writing a modern-day Hebrews 11 about people who display living faith. Whom do you know that could be included as examples of living faith? Why?

2. Imagine then that God wanted to include your life among His examples in the modern-day Hebrews 11. What could God include as an example of you living out your faith? Have you taken the first step of obedient faith, baptism into Christ? If you are not living out your faith the way you should, make an effort to start doing better. Saving faith is an active, obedient faith.

Chapter 9

WHAT ABOUT SALVATION BY GOD'S GRACE?

*"For the grace of God that brings salvation
has appeared to all men" (Titus 2:11).*

I am so thankful that God gave us a Bible full of stories from the past. From my earliest memories of Bible school, I have been fascinated with the adventures of such people as Noah, Joseph and David. As I've grown up, I've learned to appreciate even more that God decided to give us much of His Word in the form of stories. Not only are stories entertaining, but they also illustrate for us even more clearly how God works in our world. We learn what God is like. We learn what He expects of mankind. We learn from both the mistakes and the successes of the past. Sometimes the best way to understand God's laws is to look back at God's stories, which show us how the laws are supposed to work.

In this chapter we're going to let some Bible stories from the past teach us how to respond to God in the present. And as we will see, Bible stories can sometimes take complex ideas and make them simple for us. But before we get to the simple, let's begin with the complex.

An Objection: God, Not Baptism

By now it is clear that the religious world struggles with understanding how and when God has promised to give salvation. We have found answers to two of those struggles so far. First, we have seen that all of God's requirements for salvation must be followed – requirements that are brought together in the act of baptism. Second, we have seen that the commonly held idea of "salvation by faith only" is simply not biblical because faith is considered dead until it obeys. These two lessons have a common theme: We cannot stop with just one or two salvation commands but must do all that God says must be done to be saved.

With this emphasis on obedience, we might run across another voice from the religious world that sounds something like this: "You are getting it all wrong! You are focusing so much on what we must do to be saved, but the fact is that we can do nothing to save ourselves. God is the only one who can save us, and therefore we cannot be saved by any act that we perform, including baptism. Salvation is by God's grace, not baptism."

A passage of Scripture often associated with this reasoning is Ephesians 2:8-9, written by Paul: "For by grace you have been saved through faith, and that not of yourselves; it is the gift of God, not of works, lest anyone should boast."

Paul plainly reminded the Ephesians that God's grace saved them. How did it save them? Through faith, which was the gift of God, and not through works, so that no one could boast that they had saved themselves. We hear the voice again: "There you have it – we're saved by God's grace, not by anything we can do."

This objection forces us to move into the deepest waters we have explored yet. Starting in the quiet harbor of baptism passages, we saw a simple picture of what baptism is all about. Moving out into the larger waves of other salvation commands, we saw that every salvation command is important and that each is brought to fruition in baptism. Now we move still further out, into the even more difficult discussion of how God gives salvation to men at all.

If God gives us salvation by grace, is obedience unnecessary? Are we ignoring God's grace by saying that we must be baptized to be saved? How can the Bible say that we are saved by baptism (1 Peter 3:21) and also say that we are saved by grace through faith (Ephesians 2:8)? How can these various waters flow together to form one consistent sea? Before we get too intimidated by the height of the waves, let's close our eyes and go back to the simpler world of Bible school, where a few good old-fashioned Bible stories may help us.

How God Gives His Blessings

Joshua stared out toward Jericho, wondering how it would happen. He and the Israelites had just experienced God's latest miracle: The Jordan River had parted, and the Israelites had crossed through it on dry ground. For the first time in hundreds of years, God's chosen family once again stood in the land of Canaan. But there was still work to be done: Before they could call the land their own, they would have to defeat the many peoples who had come to power. The first stop on the map was the well-protected city of Jericho, which was very aware that the Israelites were *God was giving the Israelites the city. No need to try the impossible and scale the walls themselves; God was taking care of it. That, my friends, is grace.* nearby. Their gates were tightly shut, and no one was going in or coming out. Joshua must have known that the Israelites could not do this without God. How would they defeat Jericho?

Fortunately, God stepped in before Joshua was forced to design an attack plan. Read what God told Joshua in Joshua 6:2, before any attack was made: "See! I have given Jericho into your hand, its king, and the mighty men of valor."

Joshua must have breathed a sigh of relief! God was giving the Israelites the city. No need to try the impossible and scale the walls themselves; God was taking care of it. That, my friends, is grace. God was giving the Israelites something they could not earn themselves.

However, God's grace came with conditions. Read Joshua 6:2-5. What would Israel have to do before God gave them the city? They were to march around Jericho once a day for six days. Then, on the seventh day they were to march around the city seven times, the priests were to blow their trumpets and the people were to shout. At the shout, God would fulfill His promise, and the wall of the city would fall down flat.

The Israelites followed God's commands until finally, on the seventh day, the walls of Jericho fell.

Clearly, the walls of Jericho fell by God's grace – there was no way Israel could have done it themselves. However, Hebrews 11:30 adds another reason for Jericho's walls going down face first: "By faith the walls of Jericho fell down after they were encircled for seven days."

They fell by faith? I thought they fell by God's grace. Is the Bible saying that the walls also fell because the Israelites believed God? Yes. But notice that their belief was not a dead faith. It was an obedient faith, a faith that acted and did exactly what God had required. What if Israel had refused to march around Jericho, stating that because God had already promised them the city, they therefore had no need to actually do what He commanded? Would the city have fallen? Apparently not – the gift came with conditions. Fortunately, Israel's faith in God's grace came alive in obedience, and because of Israel's living, obedient faith, God gave them the city of Jericho.

So let's put this story together. First, God by His grace promised to give Israel the city. Second, however, God put conditions on His gracious gift, demanding that obedient faith be shown first. Third, at the completion of all God's requirements, the walls of the city fell. Not on the first, second or third day of marching. On the seventh. At the shout. When everything was completed, God actually gave them the blessing. I think we'll find this to be a consistent means of God's giving His blessings to man.

Another Example of Grace in Action

Years before Israel took the city of Jericho, they were wandering around in the wilderness. Yet again, as they had many times before, the Israelites complained against God. They were upset because of the long journey and began blaming God for their problems. In God's anger He sent fiery serpents among the people, and whoever was bitten by the serpents died. When Moses and the people begged God for forgiveness and help, God responded in Numbers 21:8-9:

Then the Lord said to Moses, "Make a fiery serpent, and set it on a pole; and it shall be that everyone who is bitten, when he looks at it, shall live." So Moses made a bronze serpent, and put it on a pole; and so it was, if a serpent had bitten anyone, when he looked at the bronze serpent, he lived.

Once again we see the same process. By God's grace, He gave Israel something they could not give themselves: rescue from the death caused by the serpents' bites. But once again God's grace came with conditions: When someone is bitten, he or she must look at the image of the serpent Moses made. Then, only after those bitten by the snakes had responded in full obedience, God would give His blessing: They would live.

Were they being saved by God's grace? Absolutely. But God explicitly said that His grace would not cover them until after they had responded in obedient faith. If Moses had refused to make the bronze serpent, or if the people had refused to look at it, God would have refused to give His gift of healing. God promised that His grace would save at the completion of obedience.

Still True Today

That last story is especially interesting because of what Jesus said about Himself in John 3:14-15: "And as Moses lifted up the serpent in the wilderness, even so must the Son of Man be lifted up, that whoever believes in Him should not perish but have eternal life."

Salvation through the cross of Christ comes the same way it came through the bronze serpent. By God's grace, He offers us something we can't offer ourselves: salvation from our sins. However, God's gift comes with conditions: We must believe, repent, confess and be baptized. Then, at the completion of that faithful obedience to Him, God gives us His blessing of salvation from sin.

Therefore, we open our eyes to find that the waves out here aren't quite as bad as they first looked – we just had to get the hang of them. Some familiar Bible stories have made these tough questions look easy. Are we saved by God's grace? Absolutely. We could never save ourselves. We can't even see or touch our souls, much less save them by our own power. But are we also saved by our faith that is made alive in baptism? Yes – not because of how great we are but because of God's gracious promise that in our baptism He will save us. Once again, branching further out in our study has given us an even greater appreciation for what happens in baptism. But before we can land at our destination, we must navigate a few more waves.

Discussion Questions

1. Why do you think God provided so much of the Bible in story form? Do you agree that the Bible's stories help us better understand God's laws? Why or why not?

2. How might Ephesians 2:8-9 be used in an objection to the necessity of baptism? How are grace and obedience different? How can they fit together?

3. How did grace play a role in the Israelites' taking of the city of Jericho? How did faith play a role? Was it faith only or obedient faith? When did God give the blessing?

4. How did grace play a role in the Israelites' survival from bites of the fiery serpents? How did faith play a role? Was it faith only or obedient faith? When did God ultimately give His blessing?

5. How is Jesus similar to the bronze serpent of Numbers 21? In the Gospel of Jesus Christ, can you describe the process of grace, obedient faith and blessing?

6. Read 2 Kings 5:1-14. Can you find the same process here? Was Naaman healed by grace only, by his actions only or by God's grace given at obedience?

7. Do you believe we appreciate God's grace as we should?

Personal Reflection

1. What were some of your favorite Bible stories growing up? What are some of your favorites today? What do you learn from each story?

2. Is there any way we could ever save ourselves from sin? Have you been truly appreciative of the grace God has shown us through Jesus? Thank God regularly.

3. Could you explain to someone else how grace and obedient faith are related to each other?

Chapter 10

WHAT ABOUT
OTHER BAPTISM
OBJECTIONS?

"He saved us, not on the basis of deeds which we have done in righteousness, but according to His mercy, by the washing of regeneration and renewing by the Holy Spirit" (Titus 3:5 NASB).

I f these last few chapters haven't make it clear, let's spell it out again: Many religious people do not believe baptism is important in God's plan of salvation. I wish I could explain all the reasons why. I always try to assume that others in the religious world are sincere and searching for truth, but often it seems that some people are just trying to find any reason at all to downplay the importance of baptism. It's as if their minds were closed to baptism from the beginning, which seems a far cry from the New Testament picture. John the Baptist preached baptism. Jesus preached baptism. The apostles preached baptism. Today you wonder if some preachers are preaching *against* baptism! At any rate, many good, honest people still want to know the truth about baptism, and we must be able to show them what God says about it. So in this chapter, we will consider a few more objections you are likely to hear against the importance of baptism.

The Thief on the Cross

When Jesus went to the cross, He was crucified along with two criminals, one on either side. And as if the crowd's mocking weren't enough, these two thieves added further insult by ridiculing Jesus themselves (Mark 15:32). However, Luke 23:39-43 tells us about an amazing conversation that took place between Jesus and those two men suffering with Him. Sarcastically, one of the thieves began asking Jesus if He were really the Christ, wondering why He didn't simply save all of them.

In response, the other thief changed his tune and came to Jesus' defense. He rebuked the critical thief, saying in Luke 23:40-41, "Do you not even fear God, seeing you are under the same condemnation? And we indeed justly, for we receive the due reward of our deeds; but this Man has done nothing wrong."

> *Today, many people believe that the thief on the cross is full proof that baptism is not essential to salvation.*

After defending Jesus, the thief then directed his words to Jesus, begging Him: "Lord, remember me when You come into Your kingdom" (Luke 23:42). Jesus then made the thief a promise that must have helped take away some of the pain: "Assuredly, I say to you, today you will be with Me in Paradise" (v. 43). What a promise! The thief would be saved.

At the time, the thief had no idea that he eventually would become an issue in studies about baptism. Yet today, many people believe that the thief on the cross is full proof that baptism is not essential to salvation. The argument goes something like this: "The thief was saved. The thief was not baptized. Therefore, baptism is not necessary to be saved." Is this a good reason to dismiss the importance of baptism?

Right off the bat, we notice something shaky in this argument: Where does the Bible say that the thief had *not* been baptized? John the Baptist and Jesus had been preaching baptism for more than three years by this time. It is certainly possible that the thief had been baptized in the past (although – if he had been baptized – he obviously had not lived up to that commitment very well). Let me be clear: I don't know if the thief was ever baptized. But it certainly doesn't seem smart to risk my salvation on the assumption that the thief had not been baptized. There must be a wiser way to determine whether God wants me to be baptized.

That leads us to another issue for consideration: Is the incident involving the thief a good pattern on which to base our salvation? The thief's situation was entirely different from ours. For one thing, he was talking with Jesus face to face while Jesus was physically on earth. In Luke 5:24, Jesus said that He had authority on earth to forgive sins. Jesus personally forgave several people of their sins, apparently without baptism (Luke 5:18-26; 7:36-50). However, Jesus is not on earth today, personally pronouncing forgiveness on others. Instead, He has given God's new covenant to man. And this new covenant, which the apostles later taught in its fullest form, teaches that Christ's baptism is the point at which we receive forgiveness of sins through Christ's blood (Acts 2:38, for example). The thief was living in a different time – a time when Jesus could personally forgive sins and a time before the covenant of Jesus could be brought in its completed form to the world (because Jesus had not yet died for sins).

Because we live in the age after Christ's sacrificial death, when He is no longer on earth personally, where should we look to determine if baptism is important? We shouldn't look to the thief on the cross; his place in life was too different from ours. Why not look to the people in the book of Acts? They lived after the death of Christ (just like us), *The thief on the cross has an interesting story, but he is not our pattern for salvation.* and they were taught how God would offer salvation in the era after Christ (the era we live in). What were they told? Over and over again, they were told to be baptized to receive forgiveness of sins.

The thief on the cross is just as abused today as he was during his crucifixion. Discussions about the importance of baptism for us should center on the book of Acts, not on the personal forgiveness of Jesus while on earth. The thief on the cross has an interesting story, but he is not our pattern for salvation.

Not Saved by Works

Another objection to baptism's importance comes from passages like one we studied in the last chapter, Ephesians 2:8-9: "For by grace you have been saved through faith, and that not of yourselves; it is the gift of God, not of works, lest anyone should boast."

The argument goes like this: "Paul said we are not saved by works. Baptism is a work. Therefore, baptism is not important for receiving salvation."

Once again, a glaring logical problem jumps off the page: Where does the Bible say baptism is a work? In fact, the Bible makes it clear that baptism is not the type of work Paul had in mind. Ephesians 2:9 says we are not saved by works. But in 1 Peter 3:21, Peter said we are saved by baptism. If we are not saved by works, but we are saved by baptism, it only makes sense that baptism is not a work. Look also at Titus 3:5, the verse at the very beginning of this chapter. Paul wrote that we are not saved by our righteous deeds but by a "washing of re-generation." What could the "washing" be? Does the New Testament reveal any other God-given washing besides baptism? The conclusion, then, is that Paul taught we are not saved by works but by God's mercy through baptism.

So what was Paul talking about when he said we are not saved by works? If you read the whole passage, Ephesians 2:1-10, you can better understand Paul's meaning. In verses 1-5, Paul referred to the many sins in people's lives before they are saved. Then he made it clear that we are saved by God's grace not by our works. Paul was making it clear that we cannot earn our way into heaven; the only reason we can have salvation is because God has given us a way to have it (as we discussed in the last chapter).

Imagine you spend the rest of your life doing good works for others. You give all your money to the poor. You constantly help others and teach the gospel to them. Would all those good deeds earn you a ticket to heaven? No, not even close. We are sinners and can never earn our own way to heaven. Paul wrote that we cannot be saved by our own works, but he never said there are no God-given requirements for salvation.

It seems that many people do not want to emphasize baptism because they fear doing so would imply a person is saving himself by being baptized. So let's be very clear: We do not save ourselves in baptism. God is the one doing the saving in baptism. The Bible never says that baptism is a work of trying to save ourselves. In fact, it says just the opposite: We are not saved by our works, but we are saved at the point of baptism.

Paul Wasn't Sent to Baptize

Another objection to baptism's essentiality comes from Paul's words in 1 Corinthians 1:17: "For Christ did not send me to baptize, but to preach the gospel, not with wisdom of words, lest the cross of Christ should be made of no effect."

Once again, some people struggle in trying to find an argument against baptism. They believe this verse gives them justification for such an argument. The thrust of their logic is this: "Paul said he wasn't sent to baptize. Therefore, Paul was saying that baptism isn't important."

But again the logic breaks down. If you read everything in the New Testament about Paul and everything he wrote himself, does it make sense to say that he didn't believe baptism was important? First of all, Paul wrote about the significance of his own baptism. When he told the story of his conversion in Acts 22, Paul remembered in verse 16 that his own baptism washed his sins away. Does it sound like he believed baptism was unimportant?

Second, according to numerous specific examples, Paul baptized people everywhere he went. In Acts 16, Paul was in Philippi and baptized the households of Lydia and the jailer (verses 15 and 33). Acts 18:8 tells us that many people were baptized in Corinth after hearing the preaching of Paul. In Acts 19:5, Paul baptized 12 men in the name of Jesus. When Paul preached, people were baptized.

Third, Paul's letters emphasize the importance of baptism. In Romans 6:3-4, Paul reminded the Romans that they were united with Christ's death in their baptism. In 1 Corinthians 12:13, Paul reminded the Corinthians that their baptism had put them all into the one body of Christ. In Galatians 3:27, Paul reminded the Galatians that they had put on Christ in their baptism. Does it sound like Paul thought baptism was unimportant?

Then what was Paul saying in 1 Corinthians 1:17? Once again, reading the verse in context makes it all clear. If you read the entire passage, 1 Corinthians 1:10-17, you understand the problem Paul was addressing. The Corinthians were claiming their favorite preachers rather than uniting together and claiming Christ alone. Paul responded by telling them, in my paraphrase, "Don't claim anyone but Christ, because Christ is the one who died for you, and you were baptized in His name. I'm glad I didn't personally baptize many of you, so that no one can claim that I baptized in my own name instead of in Christ's name."

The context makes it clear. Paul *had* baptized several of them, but many of the people who had been baptized had not been baptized by Paul. Apparently Paul, like Jesus (in John 4:1-2), allowed others to do the actual baptizing while he did the teaching. Therefore, when Paul said that he was not sent to baptize, he meant that his God-given role was to teach, not to do the physical baptizing himself. Was he saying that baptism was not important? Of course not. His whole life reflected just the opposite.

Final Thoughts

We have navigated some difficult waters in the last four chapters, but I hope you have gained something from the journey. We have heard the other sides of the baptism discussion in an effort to understand why many in the religious world do not take baptism at its biblical face value. We have seen that these objections to biblical baptism do not stand up under close investigation. When you are in discussions with others about baptism, listen kindly to their objections. Don't become angry or frustrated. Simply present to them, as best you can, the Bible's complete message about baptism. Present it in humility and love, just the way God would want. Present it with prayer. God willing, you may be able to show an honest soul what he or she has been missing all along.

Having passed through the objections to baptism, we find the waters calming and feel that we may reach our destination with relative ease. But where do we land now? What should we do with this (perhaps) newfound appreciation for baptism? A few questions are left to be answered – important questions that will help bring together everything we've learned. My hope is that we will have the courage and wisdom to end up where God wants us to be in our understanding of baptism. But as many sailors can attest, sometimes the landing can be the hardest part.

Discussion Questions
1. Why do you think there is such a strong objection to baptism's importance in some segments of the religious world today?

2. Do you think most of these people who object to baptism today are sincere? Is it possible to be sincere but wrong? (Read Proverbs 14:12.) What can we do to help sincere people find the truth?

3. Why do some believe that the thief's experience with Jesus on the cross is evidence that baptism is not important? Do we know the thief had not been baptized? Is the thief a good pattern for our salvation today? Why or why not?

4. Ephesians 2:8-9 says we are not saved by works. Why do some people believe this means baptism is not important? How does 1 Peter 3:21 fit with verses like Ephesians 2:9? What does Paul mean when he says we are not saved by works? Name some people who seem to do more good things than anyone else you know. Could those people earn their way into heaven by those good deeds? Does the Bible say baptism is a work of saving one's self?

5. Why do some people believe that 1 Corinthians 1:17 is evidence of baptism's unimportance? What evidence in Paul's life demonstrates his belief in the importance of baptism? What did Paul mean when he said he wasn't sent to baptize?

6. How is it helpful to us to study these objections to baptism's importance? How should we handle it when someone presents these objections to us?

Personal Reflection

1. Many people naturally hold on to whatever they were taught growing up, which perhaps explains why some people are not fully familiar with the Bible's teachings about baptism. A person should not throw out everything he has been taught, but are you honest enough to listen to other evidence and go where the Bible leads? Can we expect it of others if we won't do it ourselves?

2. Do you demonstrate a good attitude when discussing difficult matters with others? What can you do better?

BAPTISM CONCLUSIONS:
WHERE DO WE GO FROM HERE?

Chapter 11

WHAT DO I NEED TO
KNOW BEFORE
I AM BAPTIZED?

*"For which of you, intending to build a tower,
does not sit down first and count the cost, whether
he has enough to finish it?" (Luke 14:28).*

We were seated in a shaded church classroom on the north coast of Jamaica, tucked away in one of the less-touristy areas, with a breeze drifting through the windows and the Caribbean Sea as a picture-perfect backdrop behind us. I was on the island with the rest of my youth group, who held a vacation Bible school there each summer. It was a mission effort with which I had been involved for several years, but on this particular trip, God had opened even more doors than usual. Several Jamaican teenage boys had shown interest in Christianity, and after getting up the nerve to ask one of them, I had begun my first personal Bible study with a non-Christian. During the next several days, he and I met in this small classroom, getting to know each other and talking about the Bible. And that's where the question of this chapter hit me for the first time since I had been baptized years earlier.

The Bible studies were going well – better, in fact, than I could have imagined. I was using some worksheets that included Bible teachings and verses lined up for me, and my new friend seemed to agree with everything we talked about. We had talked about Jesus. We had talked about faith, repentance, confession and baptism. We had talked about the church and the goal of following the Bible as our only guide.

Considering the importance of such an event, how do we make sure someone is ready to be baptized? Perhaps you're thinking about baptism yourself and wondering if you know all that you should know.

And now, I asked the question I had long wanted to ask someone: Would you like to be baptized? To my amazement, he smiled and shook his head. Yes, he said, he wanted to be baptized. I returned his smile with a big one of my own, and we made plans for him to be baptized that evening. After saying goodbye for the afternoon, the thoughts started running through my head: Was he really ready to be baptized? Had I told him all I needed to tell him? Had I offered baptism too quickly? I ran to find our preacher to ask him what someone absolutely needed to know before being baptized.

As we begin this final section from our study of baptism, these are important questions. We have learned that baptism is the event in which God promises to give His grace to the obedient believer. Considering the importance of such an event, how do we make sure someone is ready to be baptized? Perhaps you're thinking about baptism yourself and wondering if you know all that you should know. You may be talking with a friend who is considering baptism and want to make sure you tell him what God wants him to hear. In either case, this is a critical question: What must people know before they are baptized?

It makes sense to me that we return once again to the book of Acts, where we read about the apostles baptizing thousands of people. Surely the apostles told people what they needed to hear to be baptized. And perhaps the clearest example again comes from Acts 2, where Peter baptized 3,000 souls after one sermon. That one sermon must have included the necessary prerequisites for baptism, so let's examine what Peter said.

Believe in Jesus

Most of Peter's sermon in Acts 2 was about Jesus. Peter reminded the people of Jerusalem that Jesus did amazing miracles and signs among them. He accused them of putting Jesus on the cross, although he added that Jesus went to the cross because it was God's plan. He told them that God raised Jesus from the dead, that He ascended to the right hand of God, and that He had sent the Holy Spirit to the apostles.

Peter then added the inescapable conclusion: "Therefore let all the house of Israel know assuredly that God has made this Jesus, whom you crucified, both Lord and Christ" (Acts 2:36).

Jesus is Lord! He is Lord over this earth, Lord over His people. The crowd needed to hear that. And not only did they hear it, but they also were "cut to the heart" by it (Acts 2:37). Because we believe with our heart (according to Romans 10:10), I think this verse clearly shows that before the people in the crowd were baptized, they believed what Peter said about Jesus – that He is Lord.

This example reveals the first thing we must know before we are baptized: We must first be convinced that Jesus Christ is the all-powerful, crucified, resurrected Lord. *We must first be convinced that Jesus Christ is the all-powerful, crucified, resurrected Lord.* In Acts 8, as Philip is preaching in Samaria, we read in verse 12 what happens before the people are baptized: "But when they believed Philip as he preached the things concerning the kingdom of God and the name of Jesus Christ, both men and women were baptized."

Later in the chapter, before Philip taught the Ethiopian about baptism, he first taught him about Jesus. Before Saul could be baptized in Acts 9, he had to be convinced that Jesus was God, and so Jesus met him in a blinding light on the road to Damascus. Again and again in Acts, men and women were baptized – but only after hearing about and believing in Jesus.

Still today, people must first believe in Jesus as God's Son. As Peter told the crowd, we also must tell people about the life story of Jesus – about His miracles, about His death for our sins, about His resurrection, about His return to heaven until He returns again on the last day. Before anyone is baptized, he must believe in his heart that Jesus is Lord, the Son of God.

Be Ready for a Lifelong Commitment

After the Jerusalem crowd was convinced about Jesus, they asked Peter and the apostles, "What shall we do?" (Acts 2:37). Peter's first word to them? Repent. Before they were baptized, Peter told the people they must repent.

We typically use the word "repent" only at church, so many people do not understand its meaning. To "repent" means "to turn around" or "to change one's mind." When a person repents, he changes his mind from desiring sinful things to

Was Peter saying to the crowd that they had to stop sinning and begin living perfect lives before they could be baptized? Of course not.

desiring righteous things. He feels sorrowful for his sins and commits himself to avoiding sin in the future. Was Peter saying to the crowd that they had to stop sinning and begin living perfect lives before

they could be baptized? Of course not; if we had to wait until we were perfect to be baptized, no one would ever be baptized. Repentance is a commitment to stop sinning to the best of one's ability, to begin living according to God's plan and not the world's plan. Before the people in the crowd were baptized, they needed to commit themselves to living for Christ.

When Jesus was on earth, He also taught the need for understanding commitment before conversion. In Luke 14, large crowds were following Jesus. You might think that Jesus would celebrate the large crowds, but instead He used the opportunity to tell them about the serious commitment He required from His followers. Jesus told them they must love Him more than their own families. He told them they must be willing to carry their own crosses, putting their own sinful, worldly lives to death. He told them they must be willing to give up their possessions for Jesus. He told them they must be salt to the world, an example to those around them.

In the middle of all these difficult challenges, Jesus warned the crowd to "count the cost" before they decided to follow Him:

> For which of you, intending to build a tower, does not sit down first and count the cost, whether he has enough to

finish it – lest, after he has laid the foundation, and is not able to finish, all who see it begin to mock him, saying, "This man began to build and was not able to finish"? (Luke 14:28-30).

Before you follow Me, Jesus said, sit down and think about whether you are willing and able to finish the job. And the job Christ expects is clear: a lifetime of living for Him, no matter what Satan throws in the way.

Therefore, before anyone is baptized, he must decide to repent. This doesn't mean he must get his life perfect first. It doesn't mean he must know every single commandment Jesus gave. It doesn't mean he must fully comprehend every detail of what a life commitment will mean. But it does mean he must

If we had to wait until we were perfect to be baptized, no one would ever be baptized. Repentance is a commitment to stop sinning to the best of one's ability.

understand Christianity as a commitment to live his entire life Christ's way, to change whenever he sees his life out of step with God's law.

Understand What Baptism Means

After telling the crowd to repent, Peter then told them to be baptized. But it wasn't just any baptism; he told them this baptism was "in the name of Jesus Christ" and "for the remission [forgiveness] of sins" (Acts 2:38). The crowd understood – before their baptism – that their baptism would be "in the name of Jesus Christ." They would become followers of Jesus and be united with His teachings and His blessings. They also knew their baptism would be "for the forgiveness of sins" – that God would grant forgiveness to them in this act of baptism.

Throughout the New Testament, people were told what their baptism signified before they were baptized. Paul was told that his baptism would "wash away his sins" and would be a calling on the name of Jesus (Acts 22:16). As Paul wrote his letters to the various churches, he assumed that they all understood their baptism had been "into Christ" (Romans 6:3; Galatians 3:27). In the Bible, non-believers knew what baptism meant before they were baptized.

Does this mean that someone must understand every blessing of baptism before he is baptized? No, we all learn more about our Christian blessings as we go through life. In Acts 2, Peter said nothing about the great unity that is given to believers at baptism, but this is a blessing all Christians have, according to Paul in 1 Corinthians 12:13. In Acts 2, Peter also said nothing about baptism making his listeners sons of God in a special way, and yet this is a blessing all Christians have in baptism according to Paul in Galatians 3:27.

Clearly, a person does not have to know every blessing given in baptism before he is baptized. However, the Bible shows that those being baptized did know that their baptism would unite them with Christ and the great forgiveness and salvation He offers through His death. No doubt they understood their baptism was a dividing line between the old, lost life out of Christ and the new, saved life in Christ. Before someone is baptized, he should understand baptism as a uniting with Christ and His saving blessings.

Final Thoughts

What must you know to be baptized? That question was so important to me when I was considering baptism. It was important to me when I was teaching someone else about baptism. And today, whenever I have opportunities to talk to a soul about baptism, I make sure they know the three things we have seen that people in the Bible were consistently told before baptism.

Baptism is just the beginning of a lifelong journey in a relationship with Jesus Christ.

First, you must believe in Jesus as God's Son. Second, you must realize that you are making a life commitment to live God's way. And third, you must understand that in baptism you will unite with Christ and His saving blessings. If you have these three ideas set in your mind, then you are ready to give your life to Christ.

We have seen what people in the Bible knew before they were baptized, but let's not forget that they continued learning beyond the basics. Paul's letters prove that there is still much to learn after a person becomes a Christian: Christian living, spiritual growth, church organization, worship and other tenets of faith. So we end this chapter with the reminder that baptism is just the beginning of a lifelong journey in a relationship with Jesus Christ.

Discussion Questions

1. What do you think people should know before they are baptized?

2. Why is Acts 2 a good place to find the answer to that question?

3. Read the following parts of Peter's sermon in Acts 2: verses 22-24 and 32-36. In your own words, what did Peter tell the crowd about Jesus? Do you truly believe that Jesus is God's Son?

4. What does repentance mean? Does it mean your life must be perfect before baptism?

5. Read Luke 14:25-35, in which Jesus warned the crowd to think about how much He expects from those who follow Him. What are some things that Jesus said are part of that commitment? What are some other things God will expect from someone who makes the commitment to follow Christ? (Read Matthew 5–7 for clarification about the lifestyle Christ expects of His disciples.)

6. What are some of the blessings given to us in baptism? Must we understand every blessing of baptism before we are baptized? Using Acts 2:38 and 22:16 as a guide, do you agree that people should at least understand that God is saving them through Jesus in their baptism?

7. What are some values of Christian living that still must be learned after baptism? What can churches do to help new Christians continue learning? What can you do personally to help new Christians?

Personal Reflection

1. If you have been baptized, have you grown in your knowledge of God since your baptism? If you have not grown in knowledge, what do you need to do differently? Is there someone at your church with whom you could study?

2. If you have not been baptized, what more do you think you need to understand before you are baptized?

3. I once heard a preacher say that he encourages new Christians to read the book of James five times after their baptism. James says a lot about practical Christian living, so it is a good place for a new Christian to start. Take some time to read the book of James. As you read, make a list of spiritual things you would like to do better in your life.

Chapter 12

SHOULD PEOPLE
EVER BE
REBAPTIZED?

" … one Lord, one faith, one baptism" (Ephesians 4:5)
"And he said to them, 'Into what then were you baptized?'
So they said, 'Into John's baptism'" (Acts 19:3).

A pollos was a man of incredible ability. He was the type of preacher who captivated his listeners, showing an amazing ability to tie scriptures together. I imagine Apollos quoting Bible verses one after another as the audience smiled at his amazing memory and grew from his powerful words. Notice this description of him in Acts 18:24: "Now a certain Jew named Apollos, born at Alexandria, an eloquent man and mighty in the Scriptures, came to Ephesus."

What an amazing description! He was "eloquent," and he was "mighty in the Scriptures." He was just the type of preacher who would command attention. Although Apollos was a great preacher, the Bible says that, for a while, he didn't know the entire message of Jesus. Look at what the next verse (Acts 18:25) says about Apollos: "This man had been instructed in the way of the Lord; and being fervent in spirit, he spoke and taught accurately the things of the Lord, though he knew only the baptism of John."

So Apollos was preaching about Jesus. Perhaps he talked about the miracles or the teachings of Jesus. But he also talked about the teachings of John the Baptist, and at the end of his sermons, Apollos would encourage people to be baptized into John's baptism. This baptism would commit them to be followers of John's teachings: repentance, commitment to the kingdom of God, and living holy lives. Apollos did not teach baptism into Christ because he simply had not been taught about the baptism of Jesus.

Fortunately, Aquila and Priscilla heard him preach, brought him aside privately, and taught him "the way of God more accurately" (Acts 18:26). To his credit, Apollos listened with an honest heart, and he immediately went to Corinth and began preaching Jesus as the Christ. If the letter of 1 Corinthians is any indication, Apollos had made a big impression there (see 1:12; 3:4-5, 21-22; 4:6), and now he was able to teach the whole message of Christ. However, many people in Ephesus had heard only Apollos' early sermons and had been baptized with the baptism of John only. What were they to do?

That's where Paul stepped in. In Acts 19:1-7, Paul came to Ephesus, "finding some disciples." They were 12 men who were apparently following the teachings of John the Baptist and probably the teachings of Jesus as well. Paul, as an apostle, wanted to lay hands on them and give them the miraculous gifts of the Holy Spirit, which would help them learn all of God's Word. However, when these men told Paul that they hadn't heard about the Holy Spirit, Paul asked them an interesting question: "Into what then were you baptized?" (v. 3). The baptism of Jesus had been "in the name of the Father and of the Son and of the Holy Spirit" (Matthew 28:19), so if they hadn't heard of the Holy Spirit, Paul knew they had been taught about a different baptism. The men answered that they had been baptized into John's baptism.

Notice what Paul did. He explained to them that their faith and allegiance were supposed to be in Jesus, the one John the Baptist had said would come after him. So, in Acts 19:5, "When they heard this, they were baptized in the name of the Lord Jesus."

This is the only place in the Bible that talks directly about what some call "rebaptism." The men had been baptized once into John's baptism, apparently through the preaching of Apollos. But when Paul talked with them, he told them they needed to be baptized again. Why?

Why Were They Rebaptized?

At first glance, this rebaptism may not make any sense. First, these men had been taught about Jesus and were living according to His teachings. Paul even thought they looked like "disciples" outwardly. Second, they had been baptized. The baptism of John had looked the same as the baptism of Jesus; it was full immersion in water. And just like the baptism of Jesus, John's baptism was "a baptism of repentance for the remission of sins" (Mark 1:4). These men had been baptized to *It wasn't enough for Paul that these men had been completely immersed in water, even calling it baptism. They needed to be baptized the right way, with the right purpose.*

obey God to the best of their knowledge. However, it was not the baptism of Jesus. It was not a baptism that was into Christ and into His blessings. Therefore, they needed to be baptized "in the name of Jesus Christ."

So what does this story teach us? First, this passage demonstrates that the time of John's baptism had ended. John's baptism had been part of God's plan when John was preaching, but now John was dead and Jesus had shown Himself to be God's Son. Jesus had taken center stage, and His baptism was the only one that mankind was to obey. As Paul wrote in Ephesians 4:5, there was now only "one baptism."

Second, this passage teaches us that the purpose of our baptism is important to God. Think about it: The only difference between the two baptisms was its purpose. It wasn't enough for Paul that these men had been completely immersed in water, even calling it baptism. It didn't matter that they had been baptized as an attempt to obey God. It didn't matter that they were living good lives. It didn't matter that they were trying to follow the teachings of Jesus. Despite all of that, Paul said they needed to be baptized the right way, with the right purpose.

The 12 men of Ephesus had submitted to baptism, but with a different purpose in mind. Paul's response was not, "Oh, don't worry about it" or "All baptisms are the same" or "At least you did your best." Paul said, "You need to do it God's way, with the one baptism of Jesus." These men were rebaptized because the purpose of their baptism had been different from the purpose of Christ's baptism.

"Incorrect" Baptisms

Is it possible to be baptized incorrectly today? Is it possible to go under water like everyone else but not have the right purpose in mind? Is it possible to be baptized but not "in the name of the Lord Jesus"?

Some people are baptized because a family member or friend wanted them to be baptized; the purpose was to make someone else happy.

The answer to these questions is yes. Baptism in the name of Jesus is more than just going under water; otherwise, everyone who has jumped into the deep end of a swimming pool has been baptized in the name of Jesus. Baptism is also more than going through any act involving water and calling it baptism. It is more than someone simply saying the name of Jesus over a person as he goes under water. Baptism in the name of Jesus means that one's purpose is to be united with Jesus and His blessings. Acts 19:1-5 shows us that this purpose is important to God.

As you have religious conversations with others in your life, you often will find that they have been "baptized," but their purpose in being baptized may have been very different from baptism in the name of Jesus. Some people are baptized when they go to a new congregation, with the purpose of "joining the church." Some people are baptized with the purpose of "showing a symbol" that they believe they have already been saved by Christ. Some people are baptized with the purpose of "obeying God" only. Some people are baptized for the purpose of fitting in because some of their friends also were being baptized. Some people are baptized because a family member or friend wanted them to be baptized; the purpose was to make someone else happy. None of these purposes fits the New Testament description of baptism: with the purpose of uniting with Jesus and His blessings.

What should we tell people, then, who have been baptized in sincerity but for a different reason? Do we tell them, "Don't worry about it" or "All baptisms are the same" or "At least you did your best"? I believe we need to tell them what Paul said: "You need to do it God's way, with the one baptism of Jesus." If Acts 19 tells us anything, it tells us that the purpose of our baptism is important to God. We must encourage people to be baptized for the biblical reason.

Wrong Reason to Be Rebaptized

Let's wind down this chapter with a word of caution: If someone has been baptized for the biblical reason, he does not need to be baptized again. Every now and then I will talk with someone who was baptized into Christ some time ago but since then has fallen back into a sinful lifestyle. In desiring a new start, they ask to be rebaptized. Although I appreciate their hearts and am always excited that they want a fresh start to get their lives right with God, they do not need to be baptized again. Once you've been baptized into Jesus, you get a fresh start every time you repent and ask forgiveness of your sins.

Look at the example of Simon the sorcerer in Acts 8:9-24. After being baptized, he acted in a way that showed his heart was not right before God. Did Peter tell him to be baptized again? No, he told him in verse 22 to repent and pray. God gives fresh starts to Christians through repentance and prayer. He does not ask for another baptism. Otherwise, we would all need to be rebaptized every single day!

Others may desire to be rebaptized because they have learned so much more about living a Christian life since they were baptized into Christ. The fact is, every Christian learns a lot after their baptism. Remember our discussion from chapter 11: We will not know everything when we are baptized. If we knew about Jesus, if we knew we were making a lifetime commitment,

God gives fresh starts to Christians through repentance and prayer. He does not ask for another baptism. Otherwise, we would all need to be rebaptized every single day!

and if we knew why we were being baptized, then we knew exactly what the people knew in Acts 2 when 3,000 were baptized.

It is true that some people are baptized too young before they understand their commitment or the purpose of baptism. When they realize that mistake, those people are right in being rebaptized correctly. However, we do not need to be baptized again just because we have learned more about our faith since we were baptized. God expects that we will continue learning after our baptism, and He does not ask us to be baptized again every time we have gained more knowledge.

Final Thoughts

The subject of rebaptism is a difficult one, but Acts 19 shows us that it is important not just to go under water but to be baptized with God's purpose in mind. The purpose of biblical baptism is to be united with Christ and the blessings He gives. If we or those we know were baptized with a different purpose in mind, let's hold to our paraphrase of what Paul told the men in Ephesus: "We need to do it God's way, with the one baptism of Jesus."

Discussion Questions

1. Do you think people should ever be rebaptized? Why?

2. From Acts 18:24, what kind of preacher was Apollos? From verses 25-26, what did he still need to learn? Did Aquila and Priscilla do the right thing? What about their actions is an example for us?

3. In Acts 19:1-5, what made Paul believe that these "disciples" may have been baptized differently?

4. What was the difference between John's baptism and the baptism of Jesus? When Paul found out about the baptism of the men in Ephesus, what did he tell them to do? Why?

5. Is it possible to be baptized for the wrong reasons today? What are some incorrect purposes for being baptized? What should we tell people who have been baptized for the wrong purpose?

6. If you were baptized as taught in Scripture, would you ever need to be rebaptized? How do Christians get a fresh start with God after they have sinned? Do Christians continue to grow in knowledge after they are baptized?

7. Put yourself in Paul's shoes in Acts 19:1-5. Do you think it would be difficult to tell someone that he or she needed to be baptized for the right reason? What sort of attitude would we need to have when telling that person?

Personal Reflection

1. When Paul met the men at Ephesus, he quickly found out about their spiritual lives. Do you ever have conversations about spiritual matters with those around you? Why or why not? Do you think you should talk to others about spiritual things more often?

2. Notice the attitudes of Apollos (in Acts 18:24-28) and Simon the sorcerer (in 8:20-24) when they were told they were wrong. How are they an example to us?

Chapter 13

PREACHING CHRIST
MEANS PREACHING BAPTISM

*"Go therefore and make disciples of all the nations,
baptizing them in the name of the Father and of the
Son and of the Holy Spirit" (Matthew 28:19).*

One of the true unsung heroes of the New Testament is Philip. No, not the Philip who was one of the twelve, but Philip, one of the seven – as in the seven men of Acts 6 who were given a special job to do. The 12 apostles simply did not have time to deliver the daily offering to the poor personally, so they asked the Jerusalem Christians to choose seven trustworthy men to be in charge of the task. Out of more than 5,000 Christians in the church at Jerusalem, seven men were chosen, and one of them was Philip (vv. 1-6). It was quite an honor. Philip's faith must have been obvious to everyone, and we imagine him working countless hours faithfully delivering food or money to the poor all over the city.

But Philip cared not only about the physical needs of other people but also about their salvation. When persecution began in Jerusalem and the Christians were forced to scatter out of the city (Acts 8:1-4), Philip took the opportunity to bring the message of Jesus to new places.

Philip found himself in the city of Samaria, where the Bible says he "preached Christ to them" (v. 5). As Philip shared Jesus with the Samaritan people, see how they responded: "But when they believed Philip as he preached the things concerning the kingdom of God and the name of Jesus Christ, both men and women were baptized" (v. 12).

They were baptized? Who said anything about baptism? Apparently, Philip did. In preaching the message of Jesus, Philip obviously also preached about baptism. Philip believed that preaching about Jesus and preaching about baptism went hand in hand.

Later in the same chapter, an angel told Philip to leave Samaria and go south to a desert road. God apparently had a special mission there for him. When Philip arrived at the designated place, he saw an Ethiopian eunuch – a court official for the queen – returning home after worshiping in Jerusalem. The Holy Spirit told Philip to join the chariot of the Ethiopian eunuch, and Philip did as he was told.

As he came up next to the chariot, he heard the Ethiopian reading from the book of Isaiah (they often read out loud in those days). Philip asked the man if he understood what he was reading, and the Ethiopian replied that he needed someone to help him. So Philip hopped into the chariot and noticed that the Ethiopian was reading from Isaiah 53, a prophecy about Jesus. Philip

When persecution began in Jerusalem and the Christians were forced to scatter out of the city, Philip took the opportunity to bring the message of Jesus to new places.

then did just what we would expect: "Then Philip opened his mouth, and beginning at this Scripture, preached Jesus to him" (Acts 8:35).

Again, Philip "preached Jesus" – that was his message, according to the Bible. But as Philip preached Jesus, notice the Ethiopian eunuch's interruption in the next verse: "Now as they went down the road, they came to some water. And the eunuch said, 'See, here is water. What hinders me from being baptized?' "

Where did the eunuch get the idea of being baptized? He obviously got it from Philip, who was preaching Jesus. Once again, we see that when Philip preached Jesus, he preached baptism. The two went hand in hand.

Where Did Philip Get This Idea?

Why did Philip include baptism in the message of Jesus? It certainly wasn't his own idea; baptism had deep roots in the story of Christ. It had started with Jesus Himself, who had taught baptism (John 3:22-26). That's how Jesus made disciples: by telling them to be baptized (3:5; 4:1-2). After Jesus rose from the dead, He told His apostles to go make disciples:

> Go therefore and make disciples of all the nations, baptizing them in the name of the Father and of the Son and of the Holy Spirit, teaching them to observe all things that I have commanded you; and lo, I am with you always, even to the end of the age (Matthew 28:19-20).

Jesus sent His apostles into the world to "make disciples" for Christ. He told them how to make believers into disciples: baptize them in God's name and teach them to obey Christ's commands. Jesus said it: you make people into My disciples by baptizing them. Wherever the message of Jesus went, baptism was supposed to go too.

The apostles taught that message just the way Jesus had given it to them. In Acts 2, Peter was given the chance to preach about Jesus to a Jerusalem crowd numbering in the thousands. Remember what he said they needed to do? "Then Peter said to them, 'Repent, and let every one of you be baptized in the name of Jesus Christ for the remission of sins; and you shall receive the gift of the Holy Spirit' " (Acts 2:38).

The apostles baptized 3,000 that day. The message of Jesus included the message of baptism.

It didn't stop there. In Acts 10 we read about Cornelius, who was a good, religious man (vv. 1-2, 22). God arranged for Peter to have the opportunity to preach to Cornelius and his household. Peter preached about Jesus, and God even gave the listeners the ability to speak in tongues, which demonstrated to Peter that God would accept the Gentiles into the church (10:46-47; 11:15-17). So what did Peter immediately say to this good family whom God was ready to accept? "And he commanded them to be baptized in the name of the Lord" (10:48). Peter could not end his message about Jesus without telling his listeners about the need to be baptized.

In Acts 9 the message came to Saul, who would later be known as Paul. Jesus appeared in a vision to Saul on the road to Damascus. Saul was blinded for three days afterward and sat waiting in Damascus for God's instructions. God then sent Ananias, who said to Saul: "And now why are you waiting? Arise and be baptized, and wash away your sins, calling on the name of the Lord" (Acts 22:16, when Paul later retold the story of his conversion).

"What are you waiting on?" Saul was asked. "You believe in Jesus, so let your sins be washed away!" The message of Jesus came to Saul, right next to the message of baptism.

And guess what Saul (Paul) did with that message? He taught it to others just the way it was taught to him. In Acts 16:25-34, a Philippian jailer asked Paul and Silas how to be saved. What did Paul and Silas do? "Then they spoke the word of the Lord to him and to all who were in his house" (v. 32).

I suppose there is no surprise here by now. Guess what the jailer did immediately after Paul and Silas "spoke the word of the Lord" to him? "And immediately he and all his family were baptized" (Acts 16:33). You can't preach Jesus without preaching baptism.

Therefore, when Philip included the message of baptism as part of the message of Jesus, he did it for good reason. Jesus had taught it that way and had told His apostles to teach it that way. The apostles gladly obeyed. And Philip, along with every other faithful Christian teacher, followed along. I hope that you and I will follow in the long, great tradition started by Jesus: Wherever we teach the message of Jesus, we must include the message of baptism as well. According to the Bible, the two go hand in hand.

Wherever we teach the message of Jesus, we must include the message of baptism as well. According to the Bible, the two go hand in hand.

Landing Where God Wants Us To

And so we end the long journey that began way back in Chapter 1. In Section I we launched out by studying what the Bible teaches about baptism. We learned that baptism is immersion in water, the point at which we are united with Jesus and His blessings. In Section II we found ourselves in stormier waters, considering the misunderstandings that sometimes cause the religious world to dismiss baptism's importance. Finally, in Section III, we have searched for the place where God wants us to land on some practical baptism issues – and, as we said earlier, sometimes the landing is the most difficult part. I pray we will have the courage to land where God wants us to: possessing a knowledge of the purpose and importance of baptism.

We are surrounded by many good, honest people who simply do not know the Bible's complete message about baptism. We must tell these people the same thing that was told to honest, religious people in the Bible. The heart-pierced crowd in Acts 2, the Bible-reading Ethiopian eunuch in Acts 8, the sincere persecutor Saul in Acts 9, the religious Cornelius in Acts 10, and the 12 honest-hearted Ephesian men of Acts 19 were all told the same thing: "God wants you to be baptized. And not just with any baptism. Don't simply go under water. Don't just have someone say the name of Jesus over you. Be baptized with the baptism of Jesus, a baptism that unites us with Christ. In Jesus all God's blessings are given, and baptism puts you into Jesus."

That's a message God wants the world to hear, and with the journey we've just taken, my prayer is that you and I will be better able to tell them.

Discussion Questions

1. Where do we first hear about Philip (not the apostle)? According to Acts 8:5, 12, what did Philip preach in Samaria? What was the people's response in v. 12? What does that tell us about the message of Jesus?

2. In Acts 8, the Ethiopian eunuch was reading from Isaiah 53. Why would this be a good place to start teaching someone about Jesus? According to Acts 8:35, what did Philip preach to the eunuch? What was the eunuch's question after hearing the message? What does this tell us about preaching the message of Jesus?

3. Where do you think Philip got the idea to preach baptism as part of his message about Jesus?

4. What did Jesus teach about baptism? (Read Matthew 28:19-20; John 3:5, 22-26; 4:1-2.)

5. Can you name some examples of people becoming Christians in the book of Acts? How did they do it?

6. If everyone from Jesus to the apostles to their followers taught baptism along with teaching about Jesus, don't you think we should teach it the same way today? Why do some people not teach about baptism?

7. Name some people in the book of Acts who had not been baptized but were good, honest religious people. What were they told to do?

8. Do you know any people today who are honest, religious people but have not been baptized Christ's way? What do you think God would want us to tell them?

9. Do you think it will take courage to stand up for God's teaching about baptism? Why?

Personal Reflection

1. There are five major stories about conversion to Christ in the book of Acts, and all five specifically tell about the baptisms of the individuals involved. Why not try to memorize the list of the five stories? They are: the crowd in Acts 2, the Ethiopian eunuch in Acts 8, Saul in Acts 9 (and told again in Acts 22), Cornelius in Acts 10, and the Philippian jailer in Acts 16.

2. As additional memory work, memorize some key verses about baptism: Matthew 28:19-20; John 3:5; Acts 2:38; 22:16; Romans 6:3-4; Galatians 3:27; Colossians 2:12; 1 Peter 3:21.

3. What new things have you learned about baptism in this study? Has it challenged or changed your thinking? How do you hope to use this information in the future?

www.ingramcontent.com/pod-product-compliance
Lightning Source LLC
Chambersburg PA
CBHW062002040426
42447CB00010B/1871